CLEAR

8 LESSONS ON THE THEOLOGICAL FOUNDATIONS OF FAITH

CHRIS FOLMSBEE

youth
specialties

ZONDERVAN

Clear: 8 Lessons on the Theological Foundations of Faith
Copyright © 2010 by Chris Folmsbee

YS Youth Specialties is a trademark of YOUTHWORKS!, INCORPORATED and is registered with the United States Patent and Trademark Office.

Requests for information should be addressed to:

Zondervan, *Grand Rapids, Michigan 49530*

Library of Congress Cataloging-in-Publication Data

Folmsbee, Chris.
        Clear : 8 lessonson the theological foundations of faith / Chris
    Folmsbee.
            p. cm.
        ISBN 978-0-310-27752-1 (pbk.)
        1. Christian teenagers—Religious life—Miscellanea. 2. Theology,
    Doctrinal—miscellanea. 3. Theology, Doctrinal—Poplular works. I. Title.
    BV45313.F65 2010
    248.8'—dc22   2009044725

Cover design: David Conn
Interior design: SharpSeven Design

Printed in the United States of America

11 12 13 14 15 /DCI/ 24 23 22 21 20 19 18 17 16 15 14 13 12 11 10 9 8 7 6 5 4 3 2

CONTENTS

PREFACE

Hi, my name is Chris. Even though I am older than you, married with three children, and at a different place in my spiritual journey—as we all are—you and I are quite alike. Among other reasons, we're alike because we're God's handiwork, created in God's image. God designed us for the purpose of worshipping him, and we're called to be an illustration of God's love and restoration that reveals his presence to a dark and broken world.

We're also a part of a global community of people who claim Jesus as their King while striving to live out their faith. We live out our faith by continuing to trust God more deeply each day, learning to abide in Jesus, and being devoted to do everything we can to obey God and live in his intended ways. The people around us know our faith as real when they see that our devotion to God and our love for the world are the most important elements in our lives.

This book is designed to help bring your faith into focus. It's intended to help you know who God is on a deeper level and discover for yourself what the Bible—or God's story—has to say about a variety of topics, including Jesus, the Holy Spirit, the church, sin, and a few others. This book was created to help you develop or strengthen your confidence and trust in God. And it's intended to be just one part of many in the process that helps you grapple with your faith.

Perhaps this book will help you when your faith feels complicated or difficult by assuring you that the God who sometimes permits life to be hard, who seems absent and unjust at times (during natural disasters, following a tragic death, when diagnosed with an incurable disease, and so on), and who allows questions to go unanswered is the *same* God who created you and me. And he's the same God who graciously and mercifully came to this earth in order to live with humans for a little more than three decades and then die in our place so we might live eternally with him in heaven.

You'll experience times in your life (or maybe you already have) when you'll feel as though your faith isn't real or doesn't "work" or isn't even worth pursuing. You may have questions that make you wonder if God is really out there, if Jesus is really God's Son, if being a part of the church is really worth it, and so on. Through this book, it's my desire to help give your faith a foundation that leaves room for any of the tough questions, doubt, and uncertainty you may have. You may even come to expect those moments.

Your doubts, questions, and uncertainties shouldn't scare you. In fact, they ought to cause you to love God even more, knowing that the answers to life's most difficult challenges, questions, and problems may never be found. God is a big God. If we had him all figured out and therefore didn't have questions about God and our faith, then he wouldn't be the mysterious God he is. God would also be much smaller in our minds and hearts.

Here's the deal: I want you to have a faith that rocks—a faith that deepens every day and is on display for the whole world to observe. I want you to experience God in ways that propel you to levels of love for him that you didn't even know were possible. I want you to develop a trust in God that cannot be shaken. I want you to be able to find the place of peace in your life when everything around you seems to be out of place and unsettling. I want you to find unspeakable joy in your pursuit of God.

In his book *Finding Faith: A Self-Discovery Guide for Your Spiritual Quest*, Brian McClaren uses the terms *simplicity, complexity, perplexity,* and *humility* in talking about faith. Ultimately, that's the faith I want for you—one that, while it might be simple at times and complicated and perplexing at others, in the end is a faith that leads you into the way of humility. It won't be simple or easy; the way of humility is a difficult place to find. And, to be honest, it's a place we frequently visit, rather than permanently live.

I believe this place of humility can only really be found if our faith foundation is strong enough to bear the load that comes with life. This way of humility is an approach to life that accepts

God as King, provokes us to surrender to him every day in every situation, and drives us to live a life of ongoing hope and conviction in God as our ruler.

I have three basic prayers for you. First, that this book will help you on your way to finding and following Jesus with a faith that's real and reliable. Second, that this book will be just one of the processes that helps you fall madly in love with God and that you'll be inspired to ready yourself for a life of pursuing God through other disciplines such as prayer, study, meditation, fasting, and so on. Third, that as you trek through the puzzling times of life, you'll remember the truths about God you read in this book and discover from God's Word, and be able to withstand the confusion that may come, gripping ever so tightly to a God who loves you and wants to have a brilliant relationship with you.

ACKNOWLEDGMENTS

I continue to be amazed by my wife, Gina. She lives out the theology in this book. Thanks, Gina, for your love, friendship, and support.

I am forever grateful for the influence that Dr. Floyd H. Barackman (1923–2007) had and continues to have in my life. He was a terrific writer, an excellent professor, a supportive mentor, and a wonderful human being. Much of what I've included in this book comes from the notes I took throughout my theology classes at Davis College were Dr. Barackman served faithfully for many years.

I would also like to personally thank the fine people at Kregel Publications for allowing me to use many ideas and thoughts taken from *Practical Christian Theology: Examining the Great Doctrines of the Faith,* © Copyright 2002 by Dr. Floyd Barackman. Published by Kregel Publications, Grand Rapids, MI. Used by permission of the publisher. All rights reserved.

I am deeply appreciative for the creative editorial work that my friend and ministry partner Tony Myles contributed to this book.

I am thankful to YouthFront, Inc., a wonderful community of people who support my writing activities and me as a coworker and friend.

INTRODUCTION

GETTING STARTED...

Before you dive into the following pages, I want to remind you of some key truths about our faith. As you read and interact with this book and your Bible, it's critical that you keep the following in mind.

First, You Were Created to Be You!

God knew what he was doing when he created you. You were meant to be you, I was meant to be me, and your parents and friends were meant to be who they are. Just take a look around you today and I'm sure you won't find anyone who's exactly like you. And that's the way God wants it. God wants us to be *us*! As you go through this book, I believe it's important that you not compare yourself and your spiritual status against that of anyone. You are you, and you'll only ever be you—and that's just what God wants!

Look, wherever you are on your spiritual journey today—it's okay. You might think, *But I barely know or care about God or spiritual things!* That's okay. What's *not* okay, however, is for followers of Jesus who claim God as King to stay in their current positions. God wants us to grow like a tree that's planted one day and years later is reaching toward the heavens. The whole time this tree stretches toward the heavens, it's growing! It may grow slowly, or it may grow rapidly. How quickly it grows isn't the point. The point is that it's *growing*. So remember—you are you, and it's okay to be where you are on your spiritual journey. But it's not okay to stop growing.

Second, You're a Key Part of God's Story!

You and I are valued parts of a continuing storyline—God's Storyline! Regardless of our uniqueness—actually, with our uniqueness in mind—God created us to be in relationship with him. In addition to that personal relationship, God also intends for us to play a key role in his Story.

Within this Story of God, you and I play ourselves. I can't play you, you can't play me, and neither one of us can play anyone else in this Story. But we can, as individual characters who live in community with all of humanity, play several roles.

We play the role of treasured children of God whose primary purpose is to honor and glorify him with our whole lives. As members of God's family, we're called to live a life in pursuit of godliness. We also play the role of God's chosen influencers. God has chosen us to contribute to his mission! He's created us to be exactly who we are, and God wants us to use the many great gifts, skills, and talents he created in us as we fulfill his mission. Even though God knows our weaknesses, blemishes, and sinfulness, he still chose us to be characters in his great Story. We're God's partners, handpicked to help build his church by participating in a growing movement of disciples just like us who passionately desire to make more disciples.

Finally, we're designed to love. Like Jesus, we've been called to compassionately demonstrate the heart of God to all those around us.

Third, You're Just Beginning!
This book won't answer all of your questions. It won't teach you everything you need to know. It won't suffice as the only book you'll ever need to read about God. In fact, this book is barely going to scratch the surface! It *will* provide some foundational truths about God that may or may not make complete sense to you now, after you've finished reading it, or maybe ever. Hopefully, it will push you to ask more questions about your faith, not answer all the ones you already have. I want to prompt you toward pursuing more of who God is. Please don't be content with what you learn in this book. Keep pursuing God!

GOOD THEOLOGY

Part of what makes this book helpful is that it gives you an overview of what's called *theology*. Theology is the study of God, the Christian faith, and the relationship of God and faith played out in our everyday lives. Think of theology as a practical means to knowing God and how to live according to the mission God gives us. It's during the ongoing discovery of God that we can more deeply understand what God has done for all of humanity and how we can best give our lives to glorifying him.

As you read, you'll be working your way through a very orderly look at God and the Christian faith. Your consistent interactions with this book will help you discover and examine the following aspects of theology:

> God
> Jesus
> The Holy Spirit
> Humanity
> Sin
> Salvation
> Church
> Heaven

These aspects of theology can be found throughout the Bible, and they're simply an easy way to organize our ideas and thoughts about God. God isn't simple! In fact, I believe God cannot be completely understood.

Organizing theology, as I've done in this book—and as many people a lot smarter than I am have done for years—can be extremely helpful. It must be understood, however, that the Bible isn't best understood by dissecting it and compartmentalizing it. The Bible isn't solely a collection of stories *about* God; it's the Story *of* God that reveals who God is and how we're to live. God's Story is a story of his love for us and his desire for us to live in relationship with him and others.

HOW TO USE THIS BOOK

This book has been written in a way to help guide you in each of your interactions. We call them "interactions" rather than "lessons" because this isn't about sitting down and reading something in order to gather information. It's about a living, active interaction between you and God through this book, God's Word, and various activities.

There are five sections within each interaction:

> **Consider**—offers background and relevant information for each interaction.

> **Discover**—assists you as you dig into the Bible and answer the questions.

> **Reflect**—helps you review and recap the basic ideas found in each interaction. It will also provide moments of meditation and quiet as it leads you into the Pray section.

> **Pray**—gives you a prayer or allows you to develop your own prayer that's memorable and portable—a prayer that's for along the way.

> **Immerse**—helps you move from the head to the heart and hands. This section will help you immerse yourself in the lessons God is teaching you by giving you an opportunity to practice what you're discovering each day. It will give you practical and relevant ways to express your theology in your everyday life.

After each chapter you'll find a short summary of God's Story. I'd like you to consider reading this summary after you've finished reading each chapter. I realize it may get a bit monotonous to do so every time, but it's important to do your best to keep the truths that you're learning about God in context. In other words, rather than picking verses that are scattered throughout the Bible in order to prove who God is or who Jesus is, it's essential that you remember that those verses have a greater context. That context is the overarching storyline of the Bible—God is in the process of restoring the world back to its original condition and intent.

Immediately following this Introduction, you'll find the summary that you'll read after each chapter. Go ahead and read it now and then answer the questions that follow. You may want to start a journal to record your answers after each chapter and see how your thoughts progress.

Remember...

Take your time as you go through each interaction. If it helps to do one interaction a day, then do one a day. If it helps to do one interaction a week, then do one a week. Find what works best for you. The best time of the day for you might be in the morning before school, or maybe it's during lunch, or maybe it's in the afternoon or evening. It doesn't matter when you interact. What matters is that you develop a rhythm of interacting with God and that rhythm brings about a healthy discipline and practice.

As you use this book as a tool to interact with God, God's Word, and God's mission, know that I'm praying for you. God bless you as you bring your faith into focus.

A Summary Narrative of the Bible

SEEING THE BIG PICTURE

There are a variety of ways to see the panorama of God's Story. One is to look at God's Story as a series of episodes. An *episode* is a distinct event that's a part of a greater whole—like a chapter in a book or a scene from a movie. The following episodes will give us a big picture of God's Story and allow us to see more clearly God's desire to restore his relationship with us.

CREATION → SEPARATION → PROMISE → GOD-WITH-US → DEATH TO LIFE → THE CHURCH → NEW CREATION

*The circle around the symbols represents a whole and complete relationship with God.

BIBLE SUMMARY NARRATIVE

This story begins as the Creator of all, God, was preparing the earth as a place for life. God filled the earth with plants and all kinds of creatures. The most special of these creatures were human beings formed in God's own likeness—*in God's image.*

God entrusted the humans to care for the earth and all of **creation**. God walked closely with them, showing them the best possible way to live. Under God's reign, the humans lived a life that was whole and complete.

In spite of this close relationship, the humans rebelled, choosing to live their own way over God's. Living outside of God's reign brought great consequences. Now **separated** from God, humans became subject to sickness, pain, and death.

Soon, humans spiraled out of control, acting out in selfishness and violence against one another. Determined to restore his creation, God chose a man named Abraham and his descendants to be a special **people**. God made a *covenant* with them, **promising** they would extend God's blessing and restoration to the entire world!

These special people, called the Israelites, were called to live differently, showing the world what it meant to live closely with God. God gave them a beautiful land where they enjoyed great blessings and grew into a large nation.

But it wasn't long before the Israelites chose to live their own way over God's. In their rebellion the Israelites encountered great struggles and became slaves of other nations. But God continued to give his people hope, promising to send a **rescuer** to break the power of their selfishness and rebellion.

Enter a man named Jesus. His life, teaching, and miracles all proved he was who he said he was: God's Son in human form— **God-with-us**! Jesus lived a remarkable life, always choosing to live God's way. He called people to follow him, inviting them to be a part of the "kingdom of God" and live under God's reign once again.

Jesus chose a surprising way to help humans be restored to God. Because Jesus lived perfectly, God allowed Jesus to become our substitute and take on the required punishment for all of humanity's rebellion. After suffering a brutal **death**, Jesus came **back to life** three days later and was seen by more than 500 eyewitnesses. The power of selfishness and rebellion was conquered once and for all!

Jesus challenged his followers to live as he did, and he sent God's Spirit to live inside them and empower them. This was the beginning of **the church**—a community of people across the globe who follow Jesus by living God's way and share in God's mission to restore the world.

This story continues with us. We're called to be the church—a new kind of community that'll show the world what it means to live in God's reign and return to the life we were created for.

The end of this amazing story lies ahead. Jesus promised to return to earth one day and bring about God's **new creation**.

By Michael Novelli, © 2007, Echo the Story, LLC, (www.echothestory.com).

God's reign will come in fullness, restoring all things to the way God designed them. *Until then, may we live in God's ways, giving people a glimpse of what life is like in the coming kingdom.*

QUESTIONS TO CONSIDER

- As you read or listened to this narrative, what did you picture in your mind?

- What did this summary help you notice for the first time about God's Story?

- What do you think God's Story is ultimately about?

- How is it helpful to look at God's entire Story at once?

- How does this Story continue right now? How are we a part of it?

By Michael Novelli, © 2007, Echo the Story, LLC, (www.echothestory.com).

CHAPTER 1

GOD

Interaction 1: Who Is God?

As people with a personal relationship with God, we have the honor of knowing the one true and living God. Although we can *know* God, we may never fully understand him. God is full of mystery, wonder, and awe.

God has given us special attention by providing some information about himself in the Bible. It's both our responsibility and our privilege to seek God and learn all that we can about him.

As we seek to know God, we must remember that we can learn only as much about God as he's revealed to us. Take a moment to read 1 Corinthians 2:9-10—"As it is written: 'What no eye has seen, what no ear has heard, and what no human mind has conceived—these things God has prepared for those who love him'—for God has revealed them to us by his Spirit."

What has the Spirit revealed to you about God?

If you were asked to explain who God is to a friend or family member, what would you say to describe God?

DISCOVER

The following verses hint at the nature of God and will be helpful to your discovery throughout this interaction. Take a moment to look them up. Then read them slowly and attempt to uncover and absorb something new as it relates to the nature of God or who God is.

Old Testament
Exodus 3:13-14
Leviticus 11:44-45
Isaiah 44:6
Isaiah 45:22-24
Isaiah 46:9

New Testament
Romans 11:33-34
Ephesians 1:11
2 Timothy 2:13

As you've read, the verses above indicate that God is a Person. And it's true that God exists as three distinct, simultaneous Persons (also known as the Trinity: God the Father, the Son, and the Holy Spirit), each of whom is fully divine.

The fact that God has personal features or traits like ours indicates God's personhood. But while God is very much like us, we're very far from being like God. God is uncreated. He's without material body or substance; therefore, God is spirit.

Here's where it's important to recognize that there's a difference between the spirit of God and the Holy Spirit. The spirit that makes up God is an invisible force or power, while the Holy Spirit is the third member of the Trinity. The Holy Spirit is also invisible—but he's his own being.

REFLECT

Read the following verses (with emphasis added):

No one has ever seen God, but the one and only [Son], who is himself God and is in closest relationship with the Father, has made him known. (John 1:18)

Christ is the visible image of the **invisible God**. He existed before anything was created and is supreme over all creation. (Colossians 1:15, NLT)

It was by faith that Moses left the land of Egypt, not fearing the king's anger. He kept right on going because he kept his eyes on the **one [God] who is invisible**. (Hebrews 11:27, NLT)

PRAY

As you conclude your learning for today, take a moment to write a prayer to God below. As you write, ponder the difference between God as a spirit and the Holy Spirit. If it helps you, use the following truths about God to guide your prayer.

> God is a Person.
> God is divine.
> God is uncreated and invisible.
> God is spirit.

IMMERSE

Take a moment to quiet your pace. If it helps, close your eyes and take two or three deep breaths. After you feel you've established a quiet pace, take a few minutes to write in the space provided as many truths about God as you can bring to mind from this interaction.

Interaction 2: What Is God Like?

CONSIDER

God has qualities that belong to him. These qualities or attributes of God allow us to better understand him. And a better understanding of God allows us to worship him more deeply. Throughout this interaction we'll study several of God's attributes and grow in our awareness, awe, and adoration of God.

Before we study God's attributes, however, I think it's constructive for us to pause and reflect on recent world events that cause us to be grateful for our union with God. What is it about our world that makes you thankful he's your God? List those things here:

DISCOVER

The following is a list of several of the most established attributes of God and their definitions. These attributes will help you understand what God is really like. Take a moment to look up the verse(s) beside each attribute.

Life (Jeremiah 10:10; 1 Thessalonians 1:9)	The quality of being alive
Truthful (Psalm 19:7-11)	The quality of being real
Immutability (Psalm 102:25-27)	The quality of being unchanging

Eternal (Deuteronomy 33:27; Isaiah 57:15)	The quality of being infinite in duration
Infinity (Psalm 145:3, Matthew 5:48)	The quality of being without limits
Immense (Isaiah 66:1; 1 Kings 8:27)	The quality of being spatially limitless
Omnipresent (Psalm 139:7-10)	The quality of being present everywhere
Omniscient (Job 37:16; Proverbs 24:12)	The quality of knowing everything
Omnipotent (Genesis 17:1)	The quality of being all powerful
Sovereign (Deuteronomy 10:14; Isaiah 40:15-17)	The quality of being supreme

Take a moment to reflect on the above attributes. What did you learn about God?

Considering what you know about God, what do God's attributes reveal about you and your relationship with him?

REFLECT

The Bible reveals many more attributes about God. Read the verses below while taking note of the corresponding attribute. God is—

1. Full of wisdom (Ephesians 3:10)
2. Holy (Isaiah 6:1-4)
3. Righteous (Psalm 145:7, 17)
4. Just (Isaiah 45:21)
5. Good (Mark 10:18)
6. Loving (John 3:16; 1 John 3:16-18)
7. A God who hates (Psalm 5:5; Malachi 1:2-3)
8. A God who exercises grace (Ephesians 2:8; Hebrews 2:9)
9. Merciful (Deuteronomy 4:31; Romans 11:30-32)
10. Longsuffering (Psalm 86:14-17)

Now match the above attributes of God with their corresponding definitions below. (Write the attribute next to the definition.)

Set apart: _____
Exercising unmerited favor: _____
Being and doing right: _____
Being fair: _____
Reacting against sin: _____
Being and doing good: _____
Being patient: _____
Caring: _____
Showing compassion: _____
Know-how: _____

PRAY

Draw a picture that illustrates how you see God using his attributes around you each day. Try to include at least three of the attributes you've studied. After listing the attributes, take a moment to pray using very few words. Try to focus on the three attributes in your picture. For example, you might say, "God, thanks for being a righteous, loving, and merciful God!" Repeat this prayer for five minutes, allowing your mind and heart to meditate on the greatness of God revealed in these attributes.

IMMERSE

As you move through your day, find a place where you can sit and view as much of the sky as possible. You won't be able to view the entire sky without moving your eyes, so each time your eyes move, repeat this simple phrase: "God, you are amazing! Nothing can contain you, for you are spatially limitless."

Interaction 3: What Makes God Unique?

CONSIDER

God is unlike any other god worshipped today or at any time in history. He's unique for two reasons—his unity and his tri-unity. God is a God of singularity, yet at the same time God is three Persons. God is one God because he's comprised of only one divine nature. Yet he's also three Persons because God, Jesus, and the Holy Spirit share or possess in common this one divine nature. This singular, shared divine nature establishes the Three as one God.

Before you begin this interaction, take a brief moment to reflect on the above statement about God. Does it confuse you? Is it hard to grasp? You aren't alone. God is a mystery to us all. We know God consists of three Persons because the Bible teaches that truth. What we don't fully understand is how that can be. Our limited minds make it hard for us to truly comprehend our limitless God. Yet, that's also what makes God worthy of our worship.

Ecclesiastes 11:5 states, "As you do not know the path of the wind, or how the body is formed in a mother's womb, so you cannot understand the work of God, the Maker of all things." As people of God, we cannot let the unanswered questions and mysteries of God limit our faith. Instead, they should increase and build into our faith. After all, if you and I knew everything about God, how big of a God would he actually be?

DISCOVER

In his book *Practical Christian Theology: Examining the Great Doctrines of the Faith*, Floyd H. Barackman says that the biblical doctrine of God may be summarized as follows: (1) There is one

God, (2) The Godhead consists of three Persons, (3) The Father, the Son, and the Holy Spirit are distinct, coexistent, eternal Persons, and (4) The Father, the Son, and the Holy Spirit are each God.

Let's take a look at each of these truths about the Trinity.

1. There Is One God
Deuteronomy 6:4 says, "Hear, O Israel: The LORD our God, the LORD is one." This truth is repeated throughout the Bible. Take a look at the following verses:

- Isaiah 45:5
- 1 Corinthians 8:4
- Galatians 3:20
- 1 Timothy 2:5

2. The Godhead Consists of Three Persons
Matthew 28:19 says, "Therefore go and make disciples of all nations, baptizing them in the name of the Father and of the Son and of the Holy Spirit." Read these additional verses that show God as three in one.

- Genesis 1:26
- 2 Corinthians 13:14

3. The Father, the Son, and the Holy Spirit Are Distinct, Coexistent, and Eternal Persons
In John 14:16-17 Jesus said to his disciples, "And I will ask the Father, and he will give you another advocate to help you and be with you forever—the Spirit of truth. The world cannot accept him, because it neither sees him nor knows him. But you know him, for he lives with you and will be in you." Read the following verses that also speak of the members of the Godhead:

- Psalm 2:7
- Psalm 51:10-12

4. The Father, the Son, and the Holy Spirit Are Each God

Evidence that all three Persons of the Trinity are God can be found in both the Old and New Testaments. Read the verses below.

Old Testament
The Father is God: Psalm 45:6-7; Psalm 110:1
The Son is God: Isaiah 7:14; 9:6
The Holy Spirit is God: Jeremiah 31:33-34

New Testament
The Father is God: John 6:27; Romans 1:7; 1 Peter 1:2
The Son is God: John 1:1; Romans 9:5; Hebrews 1:8
The Holy Spirit is God: 1 Corinthians 3:16; Acts 5:3-4

REFLECT

Take a moment to draw a picture that illustrates the truths you've just learned about the Trinity. If you have access to colored pens or pencils, choose three different colors. Use one of the three colors to represent one of the members of the Trinity. After you draw the picture, spend some time meditating on it. Empty your mind of all distractions and fill it with *only* truths about the Trinity. Then write a paragraph (below your picture) that explains the truths. Write it as if you're in a conversation with one of your friends.

PRAY

Write a prayer of adoration to God. In your prayer make sure to tell God how the mystery of who he is and his uniqueness result in your complete awe and wonder.

IMMERSE

Sometime today, try to explain the mystery of the Trinity to one of your friends in an email. As you do, reflect on what you've recently discovered from both the Old and New Testaments.

Interaction 4: Does God Have Any Other Names?

CONSIDER

Throughout the story of God—the Bible—we find that God has various names. When we humans use names, we typically use them to give something or someone an identity. For example, think of two or three of your closest friends. What are their names? Do they have nicknames? If they didn't have names or nicknames, how would you identify them? We use names simply to identify one another.

In the Bible, however, names are much more than identification—especially when referring to God. God's names describe his character, his nature, and his works.

DISCOVER

In the Old Testament there are three names of God that stand out to reveal his character, nature, and works: Elohim, Adonia, and Yahweh. These Hebrew names are fundamental or basic to who God is, but they're also deeply profound as they specifically relate to our understanding of God.

> Name #1: Elohim—Meaning "strength" or "might," when this name of God is used in the Old Testament, it's usually symbolic of God being the One to whom all power belongs.

> Name #2: Adonai—Typically understood to mean "Lord," this name comes from the word *Adon*, which means "master" or "ruler" in Hebrew. It can also mean "owner" or "possessor."

> Name #3: Yahweh—This name is translated "Jehovah." Although its meaning is difficult to wrap your mind around, the name Yahweh essentially means that God is

who he says he is. It comes from the root meaning "to be." God reveals himself "to be" when he says, "I AM WHO I AM," in Exodus 3:13-14.

In the New Testament we don't find the same emphasis placed on the names of God. While there's no doubt the God of the Old and New Testaments is the same God, the names used for him differ. In the New Testament, he's typically spoken of in words that we see and hear used more in our everyday language, such as *God, Lord,* or *Father.* Of course we find "Jesus," the personal name of God, used time and time again, especially in the Gospels.

Read the following verses and pay careful attention to other names of God that are used to describe his character, nature, or work.

Verse	Name
Deuteronomy 32:4	
1 Samuel 12:12	
2 Samuel 22:2	
Job 36:3	
Psalm 19:14	
Jeremiah 10:16	

REFLECT

Answer the following questions. (It's okay to look back at the "Discover" section if you need to.)

• What do we as humans typically use names for?

• What three things do the names of God help us understand about him?

• What are the three primary names of God in the Old Testament?

• What is the personal name of God in the Old Testament?

• What other names of God did you discover?

PRAY

Take a moment to slowly read the following verse five times: "The name of the LORD is a fortified tower; the righteous run to it and are safe" (Proverbs 18:10). After you've finished reading it, tell God how grateful you are that he's a "strong tower" in which you can find safety no matter what the situation might be.

IMMERSE

Carry this book, a notebook, or a journal with you throughout the day today. When you get a spare moment (you may need to *make* a moment!), try to recall as many of the names of God as you can and write them down. (Remember, it's okay to look back over the material if you need to.) As you do, choose a nearby object that might serve to remind you of each name of God.

Interaction 5: Does God Need Humanity?

CONSIDER

God loves you and the rest of humanity. How do we know this? Because God created us in his image, God provided us with a way to have a relationship with him, and God continues to show his grace and mercy to us and through us.

You might believe God doesn't need you or anyone else on this planet. After all, he's God. And after studying the names of God, it's easy to see that humanity doesn't measure up to his greatness. God is a supernatural being who has all the power and knowledge in the universe. Why would God need us?

God needs us for at least three reasons. First, he needs us to be in relationship with him. God *created* us to be in relationship with him. We were created to commune with or share life with God. Second, God needs us because we're to accomplish the purpose for which we were created—to worship and honor him. And third, God needs us to help him extend his love and blessing to the world. We're God's chosen instruments to send forth his love to a lost, broken, and needy world.

DISCOVER

What does it mean to be created in God's image? Read Genesis 1:26-27 below.

> Then God said, "Let us make human beings in our image, in our likeness, so that they may rule over the fish in the sea and the birds in the sky, over the livestock and all the wild animals, and over all the creatures that move along the ground." So God created human beings in his own image, in the image of God he created him; male and female he created them. (Genesis 1:26-27)

Simply put, to be created in God's image means that humanity was created as people, just as God is a Person. In other words, we've been created with a collection of qualities or features that distinguish us from lower creatures.

Some people believe these qualities or features include things like reason, emotion, and will. While that might be the case, one thing is certain: Humans were created to *represent* God. To be created in the image of God simply means to be like God or to be a representation of God with whatever qualities and features we've been given.

What qualities do you have that represent or serve as an image of God to others?

REFLECT

Read 1 Corinthians 10:31 five times: "So whether you eat or drink or whatever you do, do it all for the glory of God."

As images of God, what does it mean to worship and honor God?

PRAY

Lord God, help me remember that I've been created in your image.

Lord God, help me remember that I've been created to represent you.

Lord God, help me find ways today to be a representation of your love and grace.

IMMERSE

As you move through the day either today or tomorrow, do your best to be alert to the ways in which you can represent God. If it helps, make a list of all the times you find yourself thinking about being a representation. You may also want to journal about what each situation was like.

SUMMARY NARRATIVE

Take some time now to read through the Summary Narrative of the Bible on page 14 and answer the questions that follow. Repeating this exercise will help you put what you've learned in this chapter into the greater context of the overarching storyline of the Bible.

CREATION   SEPARATION   PROMISE   GOD-WITH-US   DEATH TO LIFE   THE CHURCH   NEW CREATION

CHAPTER 2

JESUS

Interaction 1: Is Jesus Really God?

CONSIDER

Jesus is known throughout the world. Even people who wouldn't claim to be Christians agree that Jesus was a real person. Most people would tell you that Jesus was born on what we celebrate as Christmas Day, that his birth divided our time from BC to AD, and that he was one of the most influential philosophers throughout the history of humanity. Many modern-day scholars and philosophers even quote him. Finding people who believe Jesus was a real person isn't that difficult. Finding people who believe Jesus was really God, however, is much more challenging. Your friends may have heard of Jesus. They may even believe he was a real person who walked the earth many years ago. But they may not believe he's also God.

DISCOVER

We know Jesus is God the Son because of his divine names, eternal existence, attributes, works, and claims. Let's look at each one of these five ideas.

1. Jesus' Divine Names
Look up the following verses.

> Matthew 1:21
> Luke 1:31-32
> John 1:1
> John 1:14
> Colossians 1:15
> 1 Thessalonians 1:10
> Hebrews 1:8

What three names do these verses give Jesus?

2. Jesus' Eternal Existence
Several passages in the Bible tell of Jesus being in existence before he was born here on earth.

> "But you, Bethlehem Ephrathah, though you are small among the clans of Judah, out of you will come for me one who will be ruler over Israel, whose origins are from of old, from ancient times." (Micah 5:2)

> [Jesus said:] "For the bread of God is the bread that comes down from heaven and gives life to the world." (John 6:33)

> [Jesus declared:] "For I have come down from heaven not to do my will but to do the will of him who sent me." (John 6:38)

> But when the set time had fully come, God sent his Son, born of a woman, born under the law. (Galatians 4:4)

3. Jesus' Attributes
Jesus, who is the express image of God (Hebrews 1:3), possesses the very same attributes of God. Some of these attributes are

listed below. Read the corresponding verses to see how these attributes are described in the Bible.

> Eternality (Micah 5:2)
> Omnipresence (Matthew 28:19-20; John 3:13)
> Omnipotence (1 Corinthians 1:24)
> Omniscience (Colossians 2:2-3)
> Goodness (Acts 10:37-38)
> Holiness (1 John 3:2-5)
> Mercy (1 Timothy 1:12-16)
> Love (John 13:1, 34)
> Grace (2 Corinthians 8:9)

4. Jesus' Works

In the Bible we find several things Jesus did that reveal he's also God. Look up the following verses and fill in the blanks below.

He was a part of _____. (John 1:3; 1 Corinthians 8:6)

Jesus _____. (Luke 5:20-25)

Like God, Jesus gives _____. (Luke 7:14-15; John 11:43-44)

Along with God, Jesus is the _____ of salvation. (Matthew 1:21; Luke 2:11; Acts 4:9-12)

5. Jesus' Claims

Jesus made some very controversial claims about who he was. Read the following verses and then write the statement or claim that Jesus is making about himself below each one.

> Then Jesus cried out, "Those who believe in me do not believe in me only, but in the one who sent me." (John 12:44)

Jesus gave them this answer: "Very truly I tell you, the Son can do nothing by himself; he can do only what he sees his Father doing, because whatever the Father does the Son also does." (John 5:19)

"I and the Father are one." (John 10:30)

What overall statement is Jesus making in the verses above?

Now read the following verses:

Then Jesus declared, "I am the bread of life. Whoever comes to me will never go hungry, and whoever believes in me will never be thirsty." (John 6:35)

"Come to me, all you who are weary and burdened, and I will give you rest. Take my yoke upon you and learn from me, for I am gentle and humble in heart, and you will find rest for your souls. For my yoke is easy and my burden is light." (Matthew 11:28-30)

What do you think Jesus is saying about himself in these verses?

Finally, read the following passage:

"My sheep listen to my voice; I know them, and they follow me. I give them eternal life, and they shall never perish; no one will snatch them out of my hand. My Father, who has given them to me, is greater than all; no one can snatch them out of my Father's hand." (John 10:27-29)

What does Jesus say he gives?

REFLECT

• Name three of Jesus' divine names.

• Name five attributes that Jesus shares with God.

• What very important works did Jesus do?

• What claims did Jesus make?

PRAY

Take a moment and write a prayer to Jesus thanking him for who he is. As you write this prayer, be as specific as you can about Jesus. Imagine Jesus is sitting next to you or across the table from you and you're looking directly into his eyes. Thank him for the things you know about Jesus.

IMMERSE

Pick one of the attributes of Jesus mentioned above. Choose an attribute that you can imagine yourself living out sometime today. In other words, can you look for a time today—and throughout this week—in which to show mercy to someone? Or can you find a way to be gracious to someone? After you've lived out one of the attributes of Jesus, take a moment to journal about the experience.

Interaction 2: Is Jesus Really God and Human?

CONSIDER

We've looked at how Jesus is God. While some believe Jesus wasn't divine but *merely* human, others believe Jesus was divine but not *really* human. Many ask, "How can someone be God *and* man?"

The answer to that question is that man cannot be God. However, God in his supernatural power can and did become human—Jesus. To be honest, I can't blame people for not believing this idea. If you think about it, this isn't an easy concept to accept. Only faith allows us to believe this truth of God, so it's especially hard for someone who hasn't yet encountered God and engaged in a relationship with him to grasp or believe it.

However, as followers of Jesus who've encountered God and decided to engage in an ongoing relationship with him, it's a critical aspect of our faith to believe that Jesus was fully God and fully human.

DISCOVER

We have faith that Jesus was not only divine but also human because the Bible tells us of Jesus' incarnation, his birth, his life, his character, and his feelings and emotions. Let's take a look at each of these aspects.

Jesus' Incarnation

The process of God becoming man is known as the incarnation. The incarnation is where God wrapped himself in flesh and took on a human nature in the form of Jesus. God took on the body, soul, and spirit of a human—just like us. Although Jesus was God, he chose to empty himself of his divine nature and live physically on earth.

> The Word became flesh and made his dwelling among us. We have seen his glory, the glory of the one and only [Son], who came from the Father, full of grace and truth. (John 1:14)

Jesus' Birth, Life, and Character

Jesus was born the same way that each of us was born. Well, not exactly. We weren't born in a stable. We were born from our mothers, however, just like Jesus. Also, it's widely understood that Jesus had a very normal life as a child and that he grew and developed just as we do.

Look up the following verses and then write next to each one the characteristic of Jesus that's also true of us.

Matthew 8:24 _____
Matthew 21:18 _____
Mark 3:5 _____
Mark 9:36 _____
John 11:35 _____
John 11:36 _____
John 12:27 _____

Jesus' Feelings and Emotions

Leading up to the events of Jesus' brutal crucifixion and death, Jesus was humiliated. Jesus felt shame and degradation as people mocked him, beat him, and even spit on him. Just like us, Jesus knows what it means to feel humiliated.

> Then he released Barabbas to them. But he had Jesus flogged, and handed him over to be crucified. Then the governor's soldiers took Jesus into the Praetorium and gathered the whole company of soldiers around him. They stripped him and put a scarlet robe on him, and then twisted together a crown of thorns and set it on his head. They put a staff in his right hand as a scepter.

Then they knelt in front of him and mocked him. "Hail, king of the Jews!" they said.

They spit on him, and took the staff and struck him on the head again and again. After they had mocked him, they took off the robe and put his own clothes on him. Then they led him away to crucify him.
As they were going out, they met a man from Cyrene, named Simon, and they forced him to carry the cross. They came to a place called Golgotha (which means "the place of the skull"). There they offered Jesus wine to drink, mixed with gall; but after tasting it, he refused to drink it. When they had crucified him, they divided up his clothes by casting lots. (Matthew 27:26-35)

How do you feel after reading the above verses?

If he were reading the above verses with you, Jesus would be feeling the same things you are.

REFLECT
- How do we know Jesus was God but also human?

- What types of things did Jesus experience in his life that were no different from what we experience throughout our lives?

- Have you ever felt humiliated? What do you think was going through Jesus' mind and heart when he was being mocked, spat upon, and beaten?

PRAY

Below, you'll find the first part of a prayer. Fill in the last part and then slowly repeat it 10 times.

Blessed are we, oh Lord, because ———————————————.

IMMERSE

Take a moment today and try to express what you've learned from this interaction. Maybe you could write a song or a poem about Jesus. Perhaps painting or sculpting might help you to remember what you've learned. Or maybe the best way for you to remember this interaction is to find someone to talk to about what you're learning. Whatever way you find most helpful, make today a day that you remember the truths you've learned about Jesus.

Interaction 3: What Makes Jesus Unique?

CONSIDER

Up to this point, we've discovered that Jesus was God *and* human. This truth is not only unique, but it's also *singularly* unique. In other words, no one else in all of history has been or ever will be both God and man!

There are other things about Jesus that make him unique—in particular, his messiahship or messianic work. Jesus' life and ministry rest on the fact that we grasp and believe by faith that he's not only Jesus, the Son of God, but also Jesus the promised messiah, "the Christ."

DISCOVER

Jesus "the Christ" or "the Messiah" are titles that simply mean Jesus is the Anointed One. Jesus was chosen to be a servant, and as God's servant—

1. Jesus served people through the power of his Father, rather than his own power.

> [Peter said:] "You know what has happened throughout the province of Judea, beginning in Galilee after the baptism that John preached—how God anointed Jesus of Nazareth with the Holy Spirit and power, and how he went around doing good and healing all who were under the power of the devil, because God was with him." (Acts 10:37-38)

2. Jesus worked in complete union or partnership with God.

> In his defense Jesus said to them, "My Father is always at his work to this very day, and I too am working." (John 5:17)
> Philip said, "Lord, show us the Father and that will be enough for us."

> Jesus answered: "Don't you know me, Philip, even after I have been among you such a long time? Anyone who has seen me has seen the Father. How can you say, 'Show us the Father'? Don't you believe that I am in the Father, and that the Father is in me? The words I say to you I do not speak on my own authority. Rather, it is the Father, living in me, who is doing his work. Believe me when I say that I am in the Father and the Father is in me; or at least believe on the evidence of the works themselves." (John 14:8-11)

3. Jesus served people as God's Anointed One, which meant he lived a public and sacred life, rather than a private secular life.

> "Isn't this the carpenter? Isn't this Mary's son and the brother of James, Joseph, Judas and Simon? Aren't his sisters here with us?" And they took offense at him. (Mark 6:3)

> "Just as the Son of Man did not come to be served, but to serve, and to give his life as a ransom for many." (Matthew 20:28)

4. As the Messiah, Jesus was anointed to serve both God and people in three important roles: Prophet, Priest, and King.

a. Jesus was a spokesman for God—a prophet. Read Hebrews 1:1-2.

According to these verses, what was Jesus' role as a prophet?

b. Jesus is a mediator or priest. He serves people by going to God on their behalf.

Read Psalm 110:4 and Hebrews 5:5-6.

What do these verses say about Jesus as a mediator or priest?

c. Jesus is our King! Jesus rules over the lives of all believers. Jesus is the head of the kingdom. Read Isaiah 9:6-7, Jeremiah 23:5, and Luke 1:31-33.

What do these verses say about Jesus' role as King?

REFLECT
• What makes Jesus unique?

• What does it mean that God "anointed" Jesus?

• What are the roles Jesus plays as Prophet, Priest, and King?

PRAY

Read this prayer aloud softly:

> Jesus, thank you.
> Jesus, you are the Christ.
> Jesus, you are the Messiah.
> Jesus, you are the Anointed One.
> Jesus, you are our Prophet.
> Jesus, you are our Priest.
> Jesus, you are our King.
> Jesus, you are the reason we have a relationship with God.
> Jesus, thank you.

IMMERSE

Draw or paint a small picture of a crown. Cut out the picture and put it in a place where you'll see it on a regular basis. When you see the crown, be sure to tell Jesus how you're going to allow him to be the King of your life.

If you want to go deeper with this, make a list of the areas in which you struggle to let Jesus reign in your life. Then, whenever you find yourself struggling in any of these areas, stop and say this simple prayer: "Jesus, you are my King. Please help me to live as though you are my King."

Interaction 4: Why Did Jesus Have to Die?

CONSIDER

Have you ever wondered why Jesus had to die so we could live forever? If Jesus was Prophet, Priest, and King—isn't that enough? Why didn't he just leave the earth prior to his brutal death and crucifixion? Couldn't Jesus just escape it all? Yes, he could have. But then he wouldn't have accomplished his mission. Let's look at why.

DISCOVER

Here are three reasons Jesus had to die:

1. The Punishment for Sin Is Death

Think back to what you know about Adam and Eve and their sin in the garden of Eden. God told them not to eat from the Tree of Knowledge of Good and Evil or what would happen? That's right, they'd surely die. God promised that humans would die from their sin. And God keeps his promises. So in order for God, in his grace and mercy, to save humanity from the death that sin brings, Jesus needed to die in our place.

Romans 3:23 says, "For all have sinned and fall short of the glory of God." A few chapters later, Romans 6:23 says, "For the wages of sin is death, but the gift of God is eternal life in Christ Jesus our Lord."

What do these verses tell us about sin?

2. The Promise from God Required an Innocent Death

Thinking back to the story of Adam and Eve and their decision to disobey God—sin—what did God do with them? That's right, God banished them from the garden of Eden. But this banishment wasn't without hope. God promised to send a sinless or innocent sacrifice to take on the punishment of sin—death.

You may already know that until Christ died for us, humans sacrificed innocent lambs to show their repentance from sin and their faith in the promise of God. Jesus was that promised, ultimate sacrificial Lamb. He was the only innocent One who could die in our place and fulfill the promise of God.

> The next day John saw Jesus coming toward him and said, "Look, the Lamb of God, who takes away the sin of the world!" (John 1:29)

> God made him who had no sin to be sin for us, so that in him we might become the righteousness of God. (2 Corinthians 5:21)

3. The Prophets Told of Jesus' Death

Between the time of Adam and Eve and the death of Jesus as the innocent, sacrificial Lamb, there were many prophets who warned of the punishment of sin and also told of the future Messiah who'd rescue humanity from their sins. These prophets spoke for God, and God keeps his promises. Jesus had to die because God promised through the prophets that he'd provide a way for people to be rescued from eternal death.

Read Isaiah 53:1-11. *Who is the prophet talking about?*

REFLECT

Think back on what you've just discovered about why Jesus had to die. If one of your friends were to ask you, "Why did Jesus have to die?" what would you say? Write your response below.

PRAY

Repeat this prayer five times. As you say it, close your eyes and imagine how Jesus is responding as he hears you pray.

Jesus, you are the reason why I'm alive.

Thank you from the bottom of my heart!

IMMERSE

Take a moment and write the names of your friends below. With which one will you share the message of Jesus either today or sometime this week? How will you share the message of why Jesus had to die? Tell someone you trust that you plan to share what you're learning about Jesus with one of your friends. Doing so will allow someone to remind you of your plan (offer accountability) and pray for you as you carry it out.

Interaction 5: What Did the Death of Jesus Accomplish?

CONSIDER

Jesus died for several reasons. We've already covered at least three of them. Do you remember what they were? Without looking back at Interaction 4, try to list three reasons why Jesus had to die.

1.

2.

3.

DISCOVER

So we know Jesus had to die and why, but what did Jesus' death really accomplish? It accomplished several things.

1. Jesus' death made it possible for all of humanity to be reconciled with God.

> But we do see Jesus, who was made lower than the angels for a little while, now crowned with glory and honor because he suffered death, so that by the grace of God he might taste death for everyone. (Hebrews 2:9)

> He is the atoning sacrifice for our sins, and not only for ours but also for the sins of the whole world. (1 John 2:2)

2. Jesus' death introduced a new covenant between God and his people.

> Now that this faith has come, we are no longer under the supervision of the law. (Galatians 3:25)

> The former regulation is set aside because it was weak
> and useless (for the law made nothing perfect), and a
> better hope is introduced, by which we draw near to
> God. (Hebrews 7:18-19)

With the death of Jesus came a new way to believe in God—
through faith brought about by God's grace. The old way of
expressing belief in God was done away with. That doesn't mean
it's not an important and vibrant part of the history of God and
his people. It simply means that the way in which we express our
faith in God has changed. With the death of Jesus came a new
way for God and man to be in relationship with one another.

3. Jesus' death laid the foundation for the hope in which we eagerly await.

> The creation waits in eager expectation for the children
> of God to be revealed. For the creation was subjected
> to frustration, not by its own choice, but by the will of
> the one who subjected it, in hope that the creation itself
> will be liberated from its bondage to decay and brought
> into the freedom and glory of the children of God.
> (Romans 8:19-21)

Jesus' death provided a new reason to live our lives—to one day
be brought into the glory of God—heaven!

REFLECT

• What does it mean that Jesus died for all of humanity?

• What is the new covenant that Jesus brought about?

• Reread Romans 8:19-21. What are we awaiting?

PRAY

This is a very well-known prayer. Jesus himself prayed it. As you say this prayer now, take a moment to pause and reflect on each line.

> Our Father (*pause*)
> which art in heaven, (*pause*)
> Hallowed be thy name. (*pause*)
> Thy kingdom come, (*pause*)
> Thy will be done in earth, (*pause*)
> as it is in heaven. (*pause*)
>
> Give us this day our daily bread. (*pause*)
> And forgive us our debts, (*pause*)
> as we forgive our debtors. (*pause*)
>
> And lead us not into temptation, (*pause*)
> but deliver us from evil: (*pause*)
> For thine is the kingdom, and the power, and the glory, for ever. (*pause*)
> Amen.
> (Matthew 6:9-16, KJV)

IMMERSE

Get an old magazine and take a moment to cut out some images of people. Cut out as many of them as you want. Afterward, lay the pictures out on a table, the floor, or another place where you can see them all at once. Once you've done this, look closely at each picture and ask yourself these questions:

1. What do I have in common with these people?
2. What does God think about these people?
3. How should God's view of them change the way I see and treat them?

SUMMARY NARRATIVE

Take some time now to read through the Summary Narrative of the Bible on page 14 and answer the questions that follow.

Repeating this exercise will help you put what you've learned in this chapter into the greater context of the overarching storyline of the Bible.

| CREATION | SEPARATION | PROMISE | GOD-WITH-US | DEATH TO LIFE | THE CHURCH | NEW CREATION |

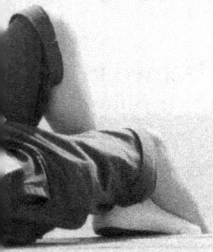

CHAPTER 3

THE HOLY SPIRIT

Interaction 1: Who Is the Holy Spirit?

CONSIDER

I'm deeply intrigued by the Holy Spirit. Whenever I read a book, hear a sermon, or have a conversation with a friend about the Holy Spirit, my interest is heightened and I want to learn more.

The nature and role of the Holy Spirit is vital to our faith. Trying to better understand the Holy Spirit can help draw us closer to God and help us to live more effectively in his intended ways. As we'll see, the Holy Spirit plays a very significant role in the life of the believer, as well as in the life of the not-yet-believer.

DISCOVER

It's important for our understanding of the Holy Spirit to grasp that the Spirit is God, and that the Spirit is a Person (in the sense of a separate personhood, not a human being). As you look at the following statements and verses about the Holy Spirit, watch for things you didn't know or things that surprise you.

The Holy Spirit Is God

1. The Holy Spirit is called God. Read the following verses and note how the Holy Spirit is God.

> Or do you not know that wrongdoers will not inherit the kingdom of God? ... And that is what some of you were. But you were washed, you were sanctified, you were justified in the name of the Lord Jesus Christ and by the Spirit of our God. (1 Corinthians 6:9-11)

> Now the Lord is the Spirit, and where the Spirit of the Lord is, there is freedom. And we all, who with unveiled faces contemplate the Lord's glory, are being transformed into his image with ever-increasing glory, which comes from the Lord, who is the Spirit. (2 Corinthians 3:17-18)

2. The Holy Spirit possesses the attributes of God. Look up the verses below. Next to each Scripture reference, write the attribute that's described in the passage(s).

Job 33:4; Psalm 104:30 _____

Psalm 139:7; 1 Corinthians 6:19 _____

John 3:5-6; Romans 8:1-2 _____

John 14:17; 15:26 _____

John 16:13; 1 Corinthians 2:10-11_____

Romans 1:4 _____

Hebrews 9:14 _____

Hebrews 10:29 _____

3. The Holy Spirit joins God in his work. Read the following verses, watching for the ways the Holy Spirit worked with God.

- The Holy Spirit was active in creation. (Genesis 1:2; Job 26:13; Psalm 33:6)

- The Holy Spirit inspired the prophets. (2 Peter 1:21)
- The Holy Spirit conceived Jesus. (Luke 1:35)
- The Holy Spirit brings about new birth. (John 3:3-8)

The Holy Spirit Is a Person

1. The Holy Spirit has features of personhood. Read the following verses, watching for the feature listed.

- Self-awareness (Acts 13:2)
- Individuality (John 14:26)
- Intelligence (1 Corinthians 2:10-12)
- Emotion (Romans 15:30; Ephesians 4:30)
- Will (Acts 13:2, 4)

2. The Holy Spirit has personal functions. Look up the verses below and write the role of the Holy Spirit next to each one.

- John 14:26 _____

- John 16:6-8 _____

- Romans 8:26 _____

3. The Holy Spirit responds personally. Read the following verses and notice the corresponding response of the Holy Spirit.

- The Holy Spirit grieves over sin. (Ephesians 4:30)
- The Holy Spirit helps us. (John 14:16)
- The Holy Spirit empowers us. (Acts 1:8; Galatians 5:16; Ephesians 1:17-19)

4. People respond in natural ways to the Holy Spirit. Read the following verses while watching for the corresponding responses of the people involved.

- The Holy Spirit is obeyed. (Acts 10:19-21)
- The Holy Spirit is lied to. (Acts 5:3)

- The Holy Spirit is blasphemed. (Matthew 12:31)
- The Holy Spirit is insulted. (Hebrews 10:29)

REFLECT

- Who is the Holy Spirit?

- How do we know the Holy Spirit is also God?

- What are some of the attributes of the Holy Spirit?

- What are some of the important things the Holy Spirit did to partner with God throughout history?

PRAY

Holy Spirit,

My life, my love, my strength.

Come to my side now and always,

In all of my doubts, questions, and trials

Come, Holy Spirit, come.

IMMERSE

Take a moment to sit outside and just listen to and feel the breeze. Even if it happens to be a cold day, let the sounds of the wind and the feeling of it hitting your face remind you that just as the wind blows every day in every direction, so is the Holy Spirit very near to you. In fact, the Holy Spirit is right beside you.

Interaction 2: How Does the Holy Spirit Relate to God and Jesus?

CONSIDER

This next interaction, I confess, might be a little confusing. I still haven't figured out the interplay between the three Persons of the Trinity, and I'm quite sure I'll never have it all figured out. People who've dedicated their lives to understanding and explaining it still come up short. So if you feel confused, you're not alone.

Because the Holy Spirit is also God, he's equal to the two other Persons who make up the Trinity—Jesus and God. These three Persons are equal because together in community, they form a singular divine nature.

However, if we were to rank the three Persons of the Trinity, it would look like this:

- God
- Jesus
- Holy Spirit

This doesn't mean that the Holy Spirit isn't as important as God or Jesus or that the Holy Spirit is any less powerful. It simply means that each Person of the Trinity has an intentional and particular role. God, Jesus, and the Holy Spirit aren't ranked by importance, but rather by the order of the initiation of their role.

So the Holy Spirit's relationship to God and Jesus is third in order of function, but it's equal in divinity. Confused? Me too...a little. But remember, that's part of what makes God worthy of our praise.

DISCOVER

The Holy Spirit ranks third in the Trinity because he comes from God and through Jesus. Read the following verses from the gospel of John. As you read, circle or underline the words that stand out to you.

> "I have much more to say to you, more than you can now bear. But when he, the Spirit of truth, comes, he will guide you into all the truth. He will not speak on his own; he will speak only what he hears, and he will tell you what is yet to come. He will glorify me because it is from me that he will receive what he will make known to you. All that belongs to the Father is mine. That is why I said the Spirit will receive from me what he will make known to you." (John 16:12-15)

Why do the words you marked stand out to you?

What about these verses helps you understand how the Holy Spirit could be equal to God and Jesus but still ranked third?

REFLECT

- Describe how God, Jesus, and the Holy Spirit are equal but ranked differently.

- Why do you believe it's important to know how God, Jesus, and the Holy Spirit are ranked?

PRAY

Oh Holy Spirit, Soul of my Soul, I love you.

Please help me to realize, believe, and live in the truth that you are the true God.

Help me to listen to and yield to you.

Take a moment and think about the areas of your life in which you haven't been good about yielding to the Spirit. Is it a sin like lust, stealing, or lying? Is it a divisive spirit? Whatever it may be, write it below and then pray the above prayer again.

IMMERSE

Sometime today or in the week ahead, log onto the Internet, go to Google's Images link and search for this: "Symbols of the Trinity." You'll probably find an image such as the triquetra below.

Print the image. After you print it, cut it out and put it someplace where you'll see it regularly (for example, a mirror, a notebook or journal, your iPod, and so on). Whenever you look at this image, simply say these three sentences: "I love you, God the Father. I love you, God the Son. I love you, God the Holy Spirit."

Interaction 3: What Are Some Symbols of the Holy Spirit?

CONSIDER

We use symbols all the time. Symbols are simply images, phrases, or singular words that represent something else. You could probably make a list of dozens of different symbols you've memorized simply from being bombarded by them every day. Maybe you'd think of the Microsoft or Apple logos or the Facebook or MySpace logos. Perhaps you'd think of the logo of your favorite college or professional sports teams. You might even think of the symbol that your church uses to represent itself or the symbol of your school mascot. Symbols are all around us; we use them to stand for, signify, suggest, or imply something.

In the space provided below, take a moment to sketch out the first five symbols that come to your mind.

Sometimes different symbols represent the same thing. There are a number of symbols used in the Bible to represent the Holy Spirit. However, these different symbols represent not only what and who the Holy Spirit is, but also what the Holy Spirit does.

The Holy Spirit can be hard to understand, but this variety of symbols can help us get a clearer picture of who and what the Holy Spirit is. We'll be taking a look at the symbols of a dove, oil, wind, and water.

DISCOVER

Read the following verses and take note of what you think the symbol of the Holy Spirit represents.

Dove

The beginning of the good news about Jesus the Messiah as it is written in Isaiah the prophet: "I will send my messenger ahead of you, who will prepare your way—a voice of one calling in the wilderness, 'Prepare the way for the Lord, make straight paths for him.'"

And so John the Baptist appeared in the wilderness, preaching a baptism of repentance for the forgiveness of sins. The whole Judean countryside and all the people of Jerusalem went out to him. Confessing their sins, they were baptized by him in the Jordan River. John wore clothing made of camel's hair, with a leather belt around his waist, and he ate locusts and wild honey. And this was his message: "After me comes the one more powerful than I, the thongs of whose sandals I am not worthy to stoop down and untie. I baptize you with water, but he will baptize you with the Holy Spirit."

At that time Jesus came from Nazareth in Galilee and was baptized by John in the Jordan. Just as Jesus was coming up out of the water, he saw heaven being torn open and the Spirit descending on him like a dove. And a voice came from heaven: "You are my Son, whom I love; with you I am well pleased."

At once the Spirit sent him out into the wilderness, and he was in the wilderness forty days, being tempted by Satan. He was with the wild animals, and angels attended him. (Mark 1:1-13)

The dove represents:

Oil

> So Samuel took the horn of oil and anointed him in the presence of his brothers, and from that day on the Spirit of the LORD came on David in power. (1 Samuel 16:13)

> But about the Son he says, ' Your throne, O God, will last for ever and ever; a scepter of justice will be the scepter of your kingdom. You have loved righteousness and hated wickedness; therefore God, your God, has set you above your companions by anointing you with the oil of joy." (Hebrews 1:8-9)

Oil represents:

Wind

> When the day of Pentecost came, they were all together in one place. Suddenly a sound like the blowing of a violent wind came from heaven and filled the whole house where they were sitting. They saw what seemed to be tongues of fire that separated and came to rest on each of them. All of them were filled with the Holy Spirit and began to speak in other tongues as the Spirit enabled them. (Acts 2:1-4)

Wind represents:

Water

Jesus answered, "Very truly I tell you, no one can enter the kingdom of God without being born of water and the Spirit." (John 3:5)

Jesus answered, "Everyone who drinks this water will be thirsty again, but those who drink the water I give them will never thirst. Indeed, the water I give them will become in them a spring of water welling up to eternal life." (John 4:13-14)

On the last and greatest day of the Festival, Jesus stood and said in a loud voice, "Let anyone who is thirsty come to me and drink. Whoever believes in me, as Scripture has said, rivers of living water will flow from within them." (John 7:37-38)

By this he meant the Spirit, whom those who believed in him were later to receive. Up to that time the Spirit had not been given, since Jesus had not yet been glorified. (John 7:39)

Water represents:

REFLECT

• What is a symbol?

• In what ways do symbols help us see not only what something is, but also what something does?

• Why do you think the Spirit was *descending* on Jesus like a dove in Mark 1:10?

- In 1 Samuel 16:13, what does the oil represent?

- What do you think streams of living water are?

PRAY

Holy Spirit, help me to look for you throughout my days.

Holy Spirit, help me to be reminded of these and other symbols of you.

Holy Spirit, help me to see these symbols of you as truth that I may learn of ways to more deeply connect with you and remain in your presence.

Holy Spirit, help me to rely on you as Dove, Oil, Wind, and Water.

IMMERSE

Take five minutes out of your day today and do two things. First, find a quiet place outside and watch, listen, and feel the wind. (If it's too cold, just sit by a window.) Let the wind be a reminder of the Holy Spirit.

Second, find a sink. Plug the drain, turn on the faucets, and allow the water to fill up the bottom portion of the sink. Stick your hands in the water and play with it. Try to capture the water in the cup of your hands. As the water seeps between your fingers and back into the sink, let the water be a reminder of the Holy Spirit.

Interaction 4: What Makes the Holy Spirit Unique?

CONSIDER

Just as God and Jesus have characteristics that make them unique, so does the Holy Spirit. The uniqueness of God, Jesus, and the Holy Spirit make them who they are and impact the things they do.

While the three Persons of the Trinity are connected with each other and may share some similarities, they also have distinct and unparalleled traits. God has certain roles in our life that are distinctly God's. Jesus has roles in our faith journey that are specifically Jesus'. And the Holy Spirit also has certain roles in our lives that are particularly the Holy Spirit's.

DISCOVER

The Holy Spirit has several roles that humans cannot duplicate. Take a minute to look up the following verses. After you've read all of them, draw a line to connect each verse with its corresponding role of the Holy Spirit.

Romans 8:14   The Holy Spirit convicts us.

Romans 8:26-27   The Holy Spirit guides us.

1 Corinthians 6:11   The Holy Sprit fills us up.

Ephesians 5:18   The Holy Spirit teaches us.

1 John 2:27   The Holy Spirit prays for us.

1 John 3:20   The Holy Spirit makes us holy.

REFLECT

- In what ways do you think the Holy Spirit prays for us?

- In what ways do you think the Holy Spirit teaches us?

- In what ways do you think the Holy Spirit convicts us?

- On a scale of 1 to 10, with 1 being very unaware and 10 being very well aware, how aware are you of the roles that the Holy Spirit plays in your life?

1   2   3   4   5   6   7   8   9   10

- If your friends were to ask how the Holy Spirit guides you in your faith journey, what would you tell them?

PRAY

Say the following prayer, repeating each line twice before moving on to the next phrase.

Come, Holy Spirit, and pray for me.

Come, Holy Spirit, and convict me.

Come, Holy Spirit, and teach me.

Come, Holy Spirit, and guide me.

Come, Holy Spirit, and fill me up.

Come, Holy Spirit, and make me holy.

IMMERSE

At some point today, find time to get a cup. It doesn't matter if it's paper, plastic, or glass—any cup will do. Go to a water source and by placing the cup either under or into the water source, fill the cup with water. In fact, let the cup overflow. Then empty the cup and repeat, watching the water spill over the sides of the cup. After you've done this several times, dry your hands and then—in the space below—write a personal prayer to the Holy Spirit that tells how much you long to be more aware of the Holy Spirit and his roles in your life.

SUMMARY NARRATIVE

Take some time now to read through the Summary Narrative of the Bible on page 14 and answer the questions that follow. Repeating this exercise will help you put what you've learned in this chapter into the greater context of the overarching storyline of the Bible.

CREATION   SEPARATION   PROMISE   GOD-WITH-US   DEATH TO LIFE   THE CHURCH   NEW CREATION

CHAPTER 4

CHAPTER NAME

Interaction 1: Where Did People Come From?

CONSIDER

What's your spin on how the world began? Was there a big bang? Did a Creator speak creation into existence? And just how old is the Earth anyway?

There's a reason everyone has an opinion about these issues, and it has little to do with carbon dating. You hear it when a friend who struggles with his or her sexuality asks you, "Why did God make me this way?" You've seen it when a marriage falls apart and you find yourself wondering if anyone will ever get it "right" (not to mention if there's even a "right" way to do it). Then there are those things you think about at night while you stare at the ceiling—things that have less to do with what you're doing tomorrow and more to do with why you're doing them to begin with.

What we're asking in all of this is what it truly means to be human. And knowing where we come from plays into that more than we realize. When we wonder how the world started, we're really asking if we're here by accident or on purpose. If we're just evolved ooze, then life has no inherent value. But if the miracle of creation is true and God's exhale created the first human being, then buried within our DNA is the "stuff of God."

Wow.

And if that's true, then what kind of humble greatness have you been born for...simply because of where you've come from?

DISCOVER
We're taking part in God's Story.

1. Before anything ever existed, our Triune God was already around.

> In the beginning God created the heavens and the earth...the Spirit of God was hovering over the waters. (Genesis 1:1-2)

> In the beginning was the Word, and the Word was with God, and the Word was God. He was with God in the beginning. (John 1:1-2)

What does it mean for you today that God existed before anything else? Think of ways that knowing this fact might change the way you think about the everyday moments of your life.

2. In all things, the spotlight is always on God.

> For from him and through him and to him are all things. To him be the glory forever! Amen. (Romans 11:36)

How have you seen humanity attempt to steal the focus away from God and aim the spotlight at itself instead?

3. Everything God creates comes from his goodness.

All things about the original Creation were noticeably good.

> Genesis 1:31
> God saw all that he had made, and it was very good.

Even the things we experience now in a broken world have a hidden goodness to them.

> Now we see only a reflection as in a mirror; then we shall see face to face. Now I know in part; then I shall know fully, even as I am fully known. (1 Corinthians 13:12)

> Every good and perfect gift is from above, coming down from the Father of the heavenly lights, who does not change like shifting shadows. (James 1:17)

If we're living in a broken version of God's original design, what do you imagine living in that original version felt like? How would colors look? Think about how it would feel to breathe that air. Along these lines, write one or two sentences describing your best guess at a couple of these experiences.

4. Out of all the good that God made, he gives special worth to mankind.

The following verses tell us that only humans were made in God's image.

> Then God said, "Let us make human beings in our image, in our likeness, so that they may rule over the fish in the sea and the birds in the sky, over the livestock and all the wild animals, and over all the creatures that move along the ground." So God created human beings

in his own image, in the image of God he created him;
male and female he created them. (Genesis 1:26-27)

He chose to give us birth through the word of truth,
that we might be a kind of firstfruits of all he created.
(James 1:18)

As you look at the list below, circle the attributes of God that are
healthy for humans to yearn for and take on themselves.

All-powerful	Loving
In control	All-knowing
Forgiving	Redeeming
Slow to anger	Creative
All-knowing	Gets the final word
Ability to decide what is or isn't sin	

God offers himself to us in intimate ways, both before and after
we broke the world. Look up these passages and write down the
unique ways God connects with humanity.

Genesis 2:7 _____

Genesis 3:21 _____

Hosea 11:1-4 _____

Mark 1:40-41 _____

John 1:14 _____

2 Corinthians 3:12-18 _____

1 John 1:1-2 _____

Revelation 2:17 _____

REFLECT

- What are your outstanding takeaway thoughts from what you just read?

- What's the value of knowing that your part in God's Story started in a good place?

- If Genesis 1–2 is the true reference point of God's ideal design, then when people use the phrase "God made me this way" to excuse a struggle with sin, how might they be misinformed?

PRAY

Think about the ways you've seen God restoring your original goodness and innocence as you grow in your faith. Write a prayer that consists only of praises to God for working in your life in these specific ways. Thank God for not only where you've already been, but also the person you've become.

IMMERSE

As you walk about your day and interact with people, take special note of the things you see in humanity that you don't see in any other part of creation. At the end of your day, spend time thanking God in specific ways for making you unique.

Interaction 2: What Role Does Humanity Play in God's Kingdom?

CONSIDER

Everybody loves a good hero, don't they? There's something about a person who decides to fight for good and to rescue those impacted by the current brokenness of the world. Whether they're stopping bullies in all their forms or dirtying their hands and knees to care for a need, the world notices it...because the world needs it.

How about when the opposite happens, though? Sometimes even when everyone agrees that the need is great, no one rises up to stand strong for what's right. These are the times when the unexpected hero within all of us considers coming out...for in order for transformation to happen in the world, a transformation must first happen inside us.

Jesus said the Good News is about the opportunity for all people to receive life and forgiveness through his cross and resurrection. But he also added that there's a present-day component of loving service and action that we're all simultaneously called to. Simply put, this is called "declaring the kingdom of God," and it happens in seen and unseen ways. A good example may come from your own life, for you may very well be on an internal spiritual journey with God right now because someone in your life had the courage to extend external love your way.

Simply by being human, you have the God-given potential to become a significant part of history and eternity. This is why all throughout the Bible we find God searching in every generation to strengthen those whose hearts are fully committed to him. Surprisingly, the Lord often calls ordinary people off the sidelines to be his top players on the field. God can create an "A" team using "B" people (and every letter that follows). How encouraging is that?

Will you be one of those people in your generation? Look around at the mess this world is in. God wants to change the world, and he's looking for young men and women who will allow that change to start in them. Are you in?

DISCOVER

The Kingdom Is Shared with Humanity as News

1. As news, we can track its early origins.

> I will make your descendants as numerous as the stars in the sky and will give them all these lands, and through your offspring all nations on earth will be blessed, because Abraham obeyed me and did everything I required of him, keeping my commands, my decrees and my instructions." (Genesis 26:4-5)

2. As news, we can prepare for it.

> "The time has come," he said. "The kingdom of God has come near. Repent and believe the good news!" (Mark 1:15)

3. As news, we can accept it or reject it.

> Jesus went through all the towns and villages, teaching in their synagogues, proclaiming the good news of the kingdom and healing every disease and sickness. (Matthew 9:35)

> When people hear the message about the kingdom and do not understand it, the evil one comes and snatches away what was sown in their hearts. This is the seed sown along the path. (Matthew 13:19)

Write down the names of the last three people to whom you tried to explain some piece of the Good News.

How easy or difficult was it for you to share with them?

The Kingdom Is Offered to Humanity to Choose

1. We can have a new permanent identity and address.

> Therefore, if anyone is in Christ, the new creation has come: The old has gone, the new is here! (2 Corinthians 5:17)

> But our citizenship is in heaven. And we eagerly await a Savior from there, the Lord Jesus Christ. (Philippians 3:20)

2. We can learn to see through the temporary world to reveal the real one.

> For we know that if the earthly tent we live in is destroyed, we have a building from God, an eternal house in heaven, not built by human hands. (2 Corinthians 5:1)

> So from now on we regard no one from a worldly point of view. Though we once regarded Christ in this way, we do so no longer. (2 Corinthians 5:16)

> But because of his great love for us, God, who is rich in mercy, made us alive with Christ even when we

were dead in transgressions—it is by grace you have
been saved. And God raised us up with Christ and
seated us with him in the heavenly realms in Christ
Jesus, in order that in the coming ages he might show
the incomparable riches of his grace, expressed in his
kindness to us in Christ Jesus. (Ephesians 2:4-7)

*This is an amazing offer. What makes it difficult for you or others you
know to choose God's kingdom daily?*

The Kingdom Is Extended to Humanity through You

1. Salvation was first offered through the Jews.

"No longer will you be called Abram; your name will
be Abraham, for I have made you a father of many
nations. I will make you very fruitful; I will make nations
of you, and kings will come from you. I will establish
my covenant as an everlasting covenant between
me and you and your descendants after you for the
generations to come, to be your God and the God of
your descendants after you. The whole land of Canaan,
where you now reside as a foreigner, I will give as an
everlasting possession to you and your descendants
after you; and I will be their God." (Genesis 17:5-8)

"Woman," Jesus replied, "believe me, a time is coming
when you will worship the Father neither on this
mountain nor in Jerusalem. You Samaritans worship
what you do not know; we worship what we do know,
for salvation is from the Jews. Yet a time is coming and
has now come when the true worshipers will worship
the Father in the Spirit and in truth, for they are the
kind of worshipers the Father seeks. God is spirit, and
his worshipers must worship in the Spirit and in truth."
(John 4:21-24)

2. Salvation is now offered through Christians.

This righteousness is given through faith in Jesus Christ to all who believe. There is no difference between Jew and Gentile. (Romans 3:22)

"But you will receive power when the Holy Spirit comes on you; and you will be my witnesses in Jerusalem, and in all Judea and Samaria, and to the ends of the earth." (Acts 1:8)

REFLECT

• What might it mean to be physically alive on planet Earth, yet "seated" in the heavenly realms?

• If heaven is described as the place of citizenship for Christians, then what does that mean about their place in life right now?

• In what circumstances in your life is it the most difficult for you to see people and situations with spiritual eyes that look past the surface?

• As you examine your life, what are four areas or activities in which you can do what's asked of you and find a way to reveal the kingdom of God to others?

PRAY

God, you've sacrificed so much so that I can have life and be at peace with you. Help me to remember what you did and please overflow out of my life to touch those around me. May I serve you this week by seeing others as you see them and serving them. In Jesus' name, Amen.

IMMERSE

Locally: What's happening in the lives of your neighbors (or neighborhood) that God is calling you to influence for his greater good? Starting today, do something about it and use the opportunity he's given you to reveal his kingdom in whatever ways are obvious.

Globally: Turn on a television and randomly scan three channels, including one news channel. What's happening in our culture that Jesus wants to impact? How might a God who's bigger than your life use "little you" to make a "big ripple" globally?

Interaction 3: What Makes People Unique?

CONSIDER

In chapter 3, we looked at what makes the Holy Spirit unique. And in chapters 1 and 2, we looked at the unique qualities of God and Jesus. It's important to know that humans are also unique creatures. Just as God, Jesus, and the Holy Spirit have certain characteristics and traits that are only theirs, we also have characteristics and traits that are our own.

Pick four of your friends or family members and write their names in the spaces provided in the table below. Now take a few minutes to write what makes each one unique when compared to the other three people you've listed.

Name:	Uniqueness:

Like our friends and family members, each of us has a "self." When we use the words *I* and *me*, we're usually identifying and revealing something about our "selves." Take a moment to fill in the blanks below.

I love to _____ on Saturday mornings.

I hate it when I have to _____ in my class.

It makes me happy when I get to _____.

It makes me sad when people say I'm _____.

It makes me laugh when I _____.

When we use words to describe ourselves, they reveal our own personal and distinct characteristics and traits. Each of the words you've used above describes certain aspects of your "self." We each have this uniqueness that makes us who we are.

DISCOVER

We all have a "self" that makes us distinct from other people. Despite our human differences, however, Christians have similarities that reveal what we share through our faith in Christ. And being a follower of Jesus is part of what makes us unique—a difference that the rest of the world can see. The Bible is very clear about this: We *should* look different from the rest of the world.

As Christians, we're all at different places within the following three areas, but they still reveal that we're different from the world around us.

> An **awareness** that God is God and we are not God.
> The ability to make the right **moral decisions**.
> The variety of ways to creatively **express** our love for God.

Read the following verses and then take a moment to name what the ideas revealed in the passages say about the uniqueness of Christ followers, as compared to those who don't yet believe in Jesus.

Awareness
Luke 9:23-27 _____

2 Corinthians 3:5 _____

Galatians 2:20 _____

Moral Decisions
Proverbs 16 _____

2 Timothy 2:15 _____

Hebrews 12:1-3 _____

Expressions
Genesis 1:26-30 _____

REFLECT
• Look back at how you described your friends' or family members' unique qualities. Now make a list of things that make you unique from them.

• In what ways are you dying to yourself to let God reign in your life?

• In what areas of your life do you have to make important moral decisions?

• In what ways do you feel most comfortable creatively expressing your love for God?

PRAY

Great, awesome, and mighty God: I lay myself at your feet.

Grant me the *ability* to see the uniqueness in me and in others.

Grant me the *desire* to embrace and celebrate the divergences in people.

Grant me the *opportunity* to go beyond my personal feelings and share with others the uniqueness you've created within each of us.

God, may my ability, desire, and action on the opportunities before me please you.

IMMERSE

As you go about the day today, find the uniquenesses in several of your friends or family members. Take careful note of what you observe. After making several observations, take a moment to share with them what you've noticed and why you're grateful for the differences.

SUMMARY NARRATIVE

Take some time now to read through the Summary Narrative of the Bible on page 14 and answer the questions that follow. Repeating this exercise will help you put what you've learned in this chapter into the greater context of the overarching storyline of the Bible.

CREATION SEPARATION PROMISE GOD-WITH-US DEATH TO LIFE THE CHURCH NEW CREATION

CHAPTER 5

SIN

Interaction 1: What Is Sin?

CONSIDER

All throughout the calendar, there are events that impact countless lives. Some are easy to spot—holidays that create traditions we all participate in—while others are a bit more masked in the way their impact ripples into our culture. On the weekend before Christmas, it's easy to see how the coming holiday is causing a lot of people to spend money on the latest craze. On the other hand, a single sporting event may create traffic problems miles away from its location, and the drivers involved won't understand why.

In a similar fashion, sin entered the world through a single event that's impacted all of creation. In the midst of a perfect paradise—and in an act of free will—mankind decided God wasn't good, his words weren't trustworthy, and people could do better on their own. Maybe these thoughts didn't consciously cross the minds of Adam and Eve, but that's essentially what sin involves—people withdrawing from God through their actions, words, and thought life because they believe there's something better.

Just like it's easy to recognize the Christmas season as a cause for increased spending, it's easy to view sin as the cause of the wrong choices we make each day. But it goes beyond that. Similar to when the distant cause of a traffic jam isn't recognized, people often fail to connect humanity's mortality with sin.

The problem isn't just that we do bad things. The problem is that apart from God—we are dead.

Dead.

Now picture a world full of dead people trying to make sense of their existence. Wouldn't you expect them to do anything they could to try to stimulate feeling into their lives—even if the way they went about it was harmful? This is the problem with sin—it leads to *more* sin...and we excuse it.

DISCOVER
Sin creates consequence.

1. Sin destroys our relationship with God.

> And the LORD God commanded the man, "You are free to eat from any tree in the garden; but you must not eat from the tree of the knowledge of good and evil, for when you eat of it you will certainly die."
> (Genesis 2:16-17)

> "You will not certainly die," the serpent said to the woman. "For God knows that when you eat of it your eyes will be opened, and you will be like God, knowing good and evil."

> When the woman saw that the fruit of the tree was good for food and pleasing to the eye, and also desirable for gaining wisdom, she took some and ate it. She also gave some to her husband, who was with her, and he ate it. Then the eyes of both of them were opened, and they realized they were naked; so they sewed fig leaves together and made coverings for themselves.

Then the man and his wife heard the sound of the LORD God as he was walking in the garden in the cool of the day, and they hid from the LORD God among the trees of the garden. But the LORD God called to the man, "Where are you?"

He answered, "I heard you in the garden, and I was afraid because I was naked; so I hid." (Genesis 3:4-10)

According to this passage, who does the hiding—God or us?

According to common opinion, who does the hiding—God or us?

What do you imagine God feels about sin compared to how we often feel about sin?

2. Sin limits our relationships with others.

And he said, "Who told you that you were naked? Have you eaten from the tree that I commanded you not to eat from?"

The man said, "The woman you put here with me—she gave me some fruit from the tree, and I ate it."
Then the LORD God said to the woman, "What is this you have done?"

The woman said, "The serpent deceived me, and I ate." (Genesis 3:11-13)

Identify the finger-pointing in this passage. Who's blaming who?

Where is personal responsibility ignored?

Who do you most identify with?

3. Sin antagonizes our relationship with creation (and procreation).

> To the woman he said, "I w ll make your pains in childbearing very severe; with pain you will give birth to children. Your desire will be for your husband, and he will rule over you."
>
> To Adam he said, "Because you listened to your wife and ate from the tree about which I commanded you, 'You must not eat of it,' cursed is the ground because of you; through painful toil you will eat of it all the days of your life.
>
> It will produce thorns and thistles for you, and you will eat the plants of the field.
>
> By the sweat of your brow you will eat your food until you return to the ground, since from it you were taken; for dust you are and to dust you will return." (Genesis 3:16-19)

How do you see these different "curses" played out in the world today?

4. Sin forces God to respond in one or more of the following ways, often at the same time.

a. God either warns us about or allows us to face the natural consequences of an unnatural choice.

> Then the LORD said to Cain, "Why are you angry? Why is your face downcast? If you do what is right, will you not be accepted? But if you do not do what is right, sin is crouching at your door; it desires to have you, but you must rule over it." (Genesis 4:6-7)

> Furthermore, just as they did not think it worthwhile to retain the knowledge of God, so God gave them over to a depraved mind, so that they do what ought not to be done. (Romans 1:28)

What role does our having access to the Bible play in God "warning us"?

Do you believe that God is required to instruct us any more than he already has?

b. God either disciplines us by adding consequences for our sins or withholds from us any additional consequences for our sins.

> So then, whoever eats the bread or drinks the cup of the Lord in an unworthy manner will be guilty of sinning against the body and blood of the Lord. Everyone ought to examine themselves before they eat of the bread and drink of the cup. For those who eat and drink without discerning the body of Christ eat and drink judgment on themselves. That is why many among you are weak and sick, and a number of you have fallen asleep. But if we were more discerning with regard to ourselves, we would not come under such judgment. Nevertheless, when we are judged in this way by the Lord, we are being disciplined so that we will not be finally condemned with the world. (1 Corinthians 11:27-32)

> Our parents disciplined us for a little while as they thought best; but God disciplines us for our good, that we may share in his holiness. No discipline seems pleasant at the time, but painful. Later on, however, it produces a harvest of righteousness and peace for those who have been trained by it. (Hebrews 12:10-11)

> Those whom I love I rebuke and discipline. So be earnest, and repent. (Revelation 3:19)

Can you track back to a time when you clearly saw the discipline of God in someone's life (maybe your own) for a sin they chose?

c. God either balances things out through his justice or blesses us beyond balance through his grace.

> The LORD God made garments of skin for Adam and his wife and clothed them. And the LORD God said, "The man has now become like one of us, knowing good and evil. He must not be allowed to reach out his hand and take also from the tree of life and eat, and live forever." So the LORD God banished him from the Garden of Eden to work the ground from which he had been taken. After he drove them out, he placed on the east side of the Garden of Eden cherubim and a flaming sword flashing back and forth to guard the way to the tree of life. (Genesis 3:21-24)

In the middle of Adam and Eve's most vulnerable moment, God chose to clothe humans in our shame and nakedness, while simultaneously removing us from what would keep us from being stuck in our sin forever. There is beauty in this moment, and yet God somehow gets a bad reputation for making us leave paradise.

Think deeply about this...have you ever been angry with God for his actions on the surface and missed the bigger picture as a result?

Use the spaces below to write down how you saw the situation and how it may have looked from God's perspective. You can write about different aspects of the same situation or different situations.

The Situation as I Perceived It   **The Situation as God Perceived It**

_____   _____

_____   _____

_____   _____

REFLECT
- What do you think about God allowing us the free will to choose or reject him?

- How would you describe the kind of relationship humanity had with God before we sinned?

PRAY
Read through Genesis 1–2 and then Genesis 3, taking note of the good place in which our story began. Thank God that we didn't start in a bad place, but a good one—a place that God makes possible again through his grace.

IMMERSE
Get out some paper and markers. Close your eyes and make a smudge on the paper using the darkest color. Now open your eyes and use the remaining markers to draw something beautiful that includes the shape of the smudge. As you do, pray about how God longs to form something beautiful in your life that doesn't deny your past but redeems it.

Interaction 2: Are There Different Kinds of Sin?

CONSIDER

Have you ever hidden from your parents or someone else in authority over you? Lots of little kids playfully do this every day, playing hide-and-seek in a store or not answering when called to dinner because they're too wrapped up in something else. There are also times when we'll hear someone calling us and we decide not to answer—even though we know we should. And even more interesting are those situations when we run away from whoever's calling us out of pure rebellion.

It's odd; but while parents may feel irritated by instances of both playful ignorance and willful rebellion, they definitely feel it more deeply when the hiding is done purposefully. It makes sense, doesn't it? In the first instance you're separating yourself without realizing it, but in the second example you're choosing to distance yourself from a person or situation you just don't want to be around. Clearly one is more offensive than the other.

What if it's the same way with sin? Does God view the actions of someone who, in her ignorance, simply follows the unnatural desires of sin any differently than the actions of someone who knows what's right and chooses to go his own way? If so, where does that leave us when we make that choice?

DISCOVER

Look up these passages and identify what the Bible specifically says God knows about us:

Matthew 9:3-4 _____

Luke 12:7 _____

Romans 8:26-28 _____

1 Corinthians 3:20 _____

1 John 3:19-20 _____

God Can Tell the Difference between Our Sins?

There are sins we do in ignorance.

> Therefore since we are God's offspring, we should not think that the divine being is like gold or silver or stone—an image made by human design and skill. In the past God overlooked such ignorance, but now he commands all people everywhere to repent. (Acts 17:29-30)

> So I tell you this, and insist on it in the Lord, that you must no longer live as the Gentiles do, in the futility of their thinking. They are darkened in their understanding and separated from the life of God because of the ignorance that is in them due to the hardening of their hearts. Having lost all sensitivity, they have given themselves over to sensuality so as to indulge in every kind of impurity, and they are full of greed. (Ephesians 4:17-19)

> I thank Christ Jesus our Lord, who has given me strength, that he considered me trustworthy, appointing me to his service. Even though I was once a blasphemer and a persecutor and a violent man, I was shown mercy because I acted in ignorance and unbelief. (1 Timothy 1:12-13)

Consider the last few times you got in trouble for something. How often are you quick to say, "I didn't know," when you actually did?

There are sins we do in rebellion.

> And let us consider how we may spur one another on toward love and good deeds, not giving up meeting together, as some are in the habit of doing, but encouraging one another—and all the more as you see the Day approaching. (Hebrews 10:24-25)

> You adulterous people, don't you know that friendship with the world means enmity against God? Anyone who chooses to be a friend of the world becomes an enemy of God. (James 4:4)

> As obedient children, do not conform to the evil desires you had when you lived in ignorance....For you have spent enough time in the past doing what pagans choose to do—living in debauchery, lust, drunkenness, orgies, carousing and detestable idolatry. (1 Peter 1:14; 4:3)

Has someone in your life ever hurt or betrayed you through a sin they consciously chose to do? What happened?

What difference did it make for you to know that they knew they were doing wrong, but did it anyway?

We're all guilty of sin. In fact, we were born into a sinful nature. God's Word tells us that the penalty of sin is death:

> Physical death: Our bodies will stop working one day. (Romans 5:12-14)

> Spiritual death: Our lives become numb to God. (Ephesians 2:1-5)

> Eternal death: Our souls are forever separated from God. (Revelation 20:14-15)

But the good news is that God desires for no one to be without knowledge of him and his forgiveness. Look up these verses and write down the different ways God makes this known:

Proverbs 27:17 _____

Isaiah 55:6 _____

Matthew 24:1-14 _____

Romans 1:18-20 _____

Romans 2:12-16 _____

1 Timothy 2:1-7 _____

REFLECT

• What might be an example of ignorant sin?

• What might be an example of wil ful sin?

• Do you believe people tend to sin more out of ignorance or out of their will? Why?

PRAY

Consider how your fellow Christians will let you down—at times accidentally and other times out of willful sin. Whether or not it's directly aimed at you, their actions will require a response from you: Condemnation or restoration, superiority or humility, separation or affirmation, and so on.

Pray for those times right now—that God would give you the attitude and wisdom of Christ. Jesus' way of knowing when to speak hard truth or tender healing is something we all need to grow into.

IMMERSE

Some people believe God views certain sins as being more severe than others, while other people maintain that "sin is sin." In a manner of speaking, both are true. One deals with the impact that a particular sin can have on other people (including the one who sinned), while the other deals with the separation sin causes between God and his people. God cares about both. Remember, God lives both inside and outside of time simultaneously. This means that while God directly feels the ripples of our rebellion, he also maintains a bird's-eye view over creation regarding all things, all places, and all times.

With that in mind, write out a confession to God regarding a sin you committed (recently or in the past). Be sure to identify both aspects of its effects: 1) The way the sin rippled, impacting people. 2) The distance the sin created between you and God.

Sample Confession:

God, when I stole that money—I made a judgment that my needs were more important than Bob's. I devalued his life, betrayed a friend, and hurt his integrity when he couldn't pay the money he owed. I'm sorry I made money more important than people. I denied you and your ability to provide for my needs. I went against something you've asked of me, and I doubted that your plans for me are good. Whether or not I realized it at the time, I was telling you that I was better off on my own and it made it harder and harder for me to read your Word or worship you fully... please forgive me.

Your Confession:

Interaction 3: How Can the Follower of Jesus Have Victory over Sin?

CONSIDER

Have you ever been around adults who knew you when you were younger? It seems like there's always someone at a family reunion or a friend of your parents who loves to remind you of how little you used to be (or "that one time" when you did something really embarrassing). Maybe they mean well, but sometimes it can be irritating to be boxed in by someone's perception of our present identity that's based on the past.

There are lots of things like this that can slant how we view ourselves, but sin is absolutely the worst. The memory of what we've done haunts us, damaging how others view us and what we see when we look in the mirror. Even if we've moved on from the sin, we can still bump into people who knew us when we were active in it. For some of us, this starts the cycle all over again because even *we* can't seem to get past the past.

Maybe someone's memory of who you used to be is true, but that doesn't mean it needs to be true of you for the rest of your life. It's like one of those temporary nametags you wear at family reunions—they're sticky and they say things about you, but they aren't meant to stay on you for the rest of your life.

We serve a God who's conquered death and makes it possible for us to become new creations—not just sinners in recovery, but an actual transformation.

DISCOVER

Read Acts 9:1-31 to learn about Saul's conversion experience and the way the early church (that he'd been persecuting) reacted.

What was Saul's initial reaction to God?

What was the church's initial reaction to Saul's conversion?

Sin isn't meant to be a part of our lives. But God doesn't leave us alone to wrestle with the reality that it is. Look at the verses below to discover how God commands, empowers, and educates us in regard to sin.

1. God commands us to turn away from our sins.

> "Speak to the entire assembly of Israel and say to them: 'Be holy because I, the LORD your God, am holy.'" (Leviticus 19:2)

> From that time on Jesus began to preach, "Repent, for the kingdom of heaven has come near." (Matthew 4:17)

> Come back to your senses as you ought, and stop sinning; for there are some who are ignorant of God—I say this to your shame. (1 Corinthians 15:34)

Do you believe it's possible for you to live a life that isn't stuck in sin? Explain.

2. God empowers us to turn away from our sins.

What do the following verses reveal about how God empowers us through Jesus Christ?

> John 1:12
> John 15:5
> Romans 5:1
> Romans 8:1-2
> 1 Corinthians 12:27
> Philippians 4:13
> Colossians 2:9-10
> 1 John 5:18

Why might it be a good thing to have a healthy understanding of your identity when it comes to resisting sin?

3. God educates us to turn away from our sins.

Come back to your senses as you ought, and stop sinning; for there are some who are ignorant of God—I say this to your shame. (1 Corinthians 15:34)

Since, then, you have been raised with Christ, set your hearts on things above, where Christ is seated at the right hand of God. Set your minds on things above, not on earthly things. For you died, and your life is now hidden with Christ in God. When Christ, who is your life, appears, then you also will appear with him in glory.

Put to death, therefore, whatever belongs to your earthly nature: sexual immorality, impurity, lust, evil desires and greed, which is idolatry. Because of these, the wrath of God is coming. You used to walk in these ways, in the life you once lived. But now you must rid yourselves of all such things as these: anger, rage, malice, slander, and filthy language from your lips. Do not lie to each other, since you have taken off your old self with its practices and have put on the new self, which is being renewed in knowledge in the image of its Creator. (Colossians 3:1-10)

Submit yourselves, then, to God. Resist the devil, and he will flee from you. (James 4:7)

The Bible uses strong words like "put to death" and "flee" when it comes to sin. Do you see the average Christian doing this? Or do most of us flirt with sin more than we ought to?

REFLECT

- Every time you're tempted to sin, what decisions might run through your brain?

- Do you get the sense that we tackle sin on our own or with God?

- What does this look like when it's lived out?

- How might remembering God's goodness help you choose to say no to sin?

PRAY

God, I want to live a life that's in total freedom from sin, but I know I can't do that apart from you. Guide me when I'm tempted, so I can say YES to you and NO to sin more quickly than I did the day before. In Jesus' name, Amen.

IMMERSE

Reread Colossians 3:1-10, taking special note of the things we're told to "put to death." List them below, citing an example of what it looks like to do that in a practical way. Example: Sexual immorality—I won't watch any movies that promote premarital sex.

SUMMARY NARRATIVE

Take some time now to read through the Summary Narrative of the Bible on page 14 and answer the questions that follow. Repeating this exercise will help you put what you've learned in this chapter into the greater context of the overarching storyline of the Bible.

CREATION → SEPARATION → PROMISE → GOD-WITH-US → DEATH TO LIFE → THE CHURCH → NEW CREATION

CHAPTER # 6

CHAPTER # 6

CHAPTER NAME

CHAPTER NAME

Interaction 1: What Is Salvation?

CONSIDER

It's absolutely wild how often you'll see someone taking a picture in a random public place. Maybe it's because the digital age allows for endless amounts of storage to keep our photos without any real expense. But this wasn't always the case. Back when people used standard cameras and had to buy film and then spend more money to have it developed, they were a bit more selective about snapping pictures. These cameras didn't have a mini screen that immediately showed you whether or not the picture was good. So people typically took multiple pictures of someone (or something) only if it was really important and they wanted to be sure they got at least one good photograph.

Over the years I've seen many people treat the issue of salvation this same way. Maybe they pray a certain prayer to God—with great sincerity—during a church service, only to find they're struggling with the same old sins later in the week. Suddenly doubt runs through their minds, so they pray the same prayer again the next week, and the next week, and the next. They truly want a relationship with God, yet their life's circumstances cause them to feel as though the ideal picture of them with God didn't turn out.

Interestingly, other people are just the opposite. They believe once they've prayed a prayer, they're "done" and can now do whatever they want. That would be like you posing for a great photo of you smiling with your family, but then treating them all horribly right after the picture was taken—and for the rest of the week. Which situation best captures the reality of that family's relationship—the photo with the fake smile or the disharmony afterward?

God didn't want us to have to guess about where we stand with him, so he offered a very clear Way to show us the Truth that offers us Life. Through Jesus Christ we get not only a "picture" of what God is like, but also a "snapshot" of the life he envisions for us. The good news is that we don't have to wait until we get to heaven to understand what's developing in our lives right now.

Wherever you are with God today, it's my hope that by the time you've finished reading this chapter, you'll have taken in the fullness of the "big picture" so you can not only enjoy a confident relationship as a child of God, but also explain it to others clearly.

DISCOVER

Using Genesis 1–3 as a reference, put the following events in the correct order:

_____ Humanity chooses to sin and doubt God.

_____ God makes the world.

_____ Man and woman are created.

_____ People enjoy a good, pure relationship with God.

_____ God exists.

_____ Generations of people are born into sin.

Now take a look at what the Bible says that means for us.

Salvation Is Initiated by God

1. We start out in life disconnected from God.

For all have sinned and fall short of the glory of God. (Romans 3:23)

For if, by the trespass of the one man, death reigned through that one man, how much more will those who receive God's abundant provision of grace and of the gift of righteousness reign in life through the one man, Jesus Christ! (Romans 5:17)

Some believe people are born innocent. But according to Scripture, **all** *have sinned. Why do we want to believe otherwise?*

2. On our own we remain disconnected from God.

All of us have become like one who is unclean, and all our righteous acts are like filthy rags; we all shrivel up like a leaf, and like the wind our sins sweep us away. (Isaiah 64:6)

For the wages of sin is death. (Romans 6:23)

When have you been unable to change something in your own power? Describe that time.

How did this make you feel?

3. God chose to be reconnected with us.

But the gift of God is eternal life in Christ Jesus our Lord. (Romans 6:23)

> But when the set time had fully come, God sent his Son, born of a woman, born under the law, to redeem those under the law, that we might receive adoption to sonship. Because you are his sons, God sent the Spirit of his Son into our hearts, the Spirit who calls out, "*Abba*, Father." So you are no longer slaves, but God's children; and since you are his children, he has made you also heirs. (Galatians 4:4-7)

Notice how God models both justice and grace in this act—

> Justice: "Someone must pay for the sin that separates us."

> Grace: "I will pay for the sin that separates us."

4. We can start a new life reconnected with God.

> So from now on we regard no one from a worldly point of view. Though we once regarded Christ in this way, we do so no longer. Therefore, if anyone is in Christ, the new creation has come: The old has gone, the new is here! (2 Corinthians 5:16-17)

> Once you were alienated from God and were enemies in your minds because of your evil behavior. But now he has reconciled you by Christ's physical body through death to present you holy in his sight, without blemish and free from accusation— if you continue in your faith, established and firm, and do not move from the hope held out in the gospel. This is the gospel that you heard and that has been proclaimed to every creature under heaven, and of which I, Paul, have become a servant. (Colossians 1:21-23)

> For you have been born again, not of perishable seed, but of imperishable, through the living and enduring word of God. (1 Peter 1:23)

In the previous verses, underline the words that stand out to you about the new identity we're given through Jesus Christ.

REFLECT

• How does one receive salvation? By growing up in a Christian home? By attending church? Something else?

• There are lots of religions in the world through which people believe they can earn eternal life on their own. What might be the appeal of a belief system in which people don't need God to save them?

PRAY

God, who am I that you'd walk into dark places for me? You have every right to leave me stuck in my sin, yet you've journeyed to be with me so I can be with you. Please help me to take your hand today—and every day—trusting in the confidence that "you've got me and I've got you." In Jesus' name, Amen.

IMMERSE

Take a moment and write down your expectation for salvation— what it means to be "saved." What part of salvation do you expect to experience in your daily life? In your eternal life?

Interaction 2: What Are the Components of Salvation?

CONSIDER

Let's settle this issue once and for all: If you're in a hurry, should you take a main road or a back road? While the main road is paved, there's a greater risk you'll encounter (get stuck behind) other vehicles. Less-traveled roads may seem like a better option because they don't have traffic lights. But on the flip side, if you get stuck in the mud, it may be difficult to find help.

This discussion may seem pointless, but consider where your mind goes when you first consider the question. Chances are if you're a "main road" person, you'll give someone directions based on that preference. On the other hand, if you enjoy cruising down country lanes, then you'll be more likely to tell someone *that's* the best way to travel. We tend to give directions based on our own experiences and preferences.

Now imagine if someone were to ask you how he can "get saved" like you are. Would you give him instructions based on your own journey? Or would you lean in and hear what God is stirring in his heart? This is a question that Jesus was familiar with during his ministry on earth, because while people came to him from different circumstances, they all desired the same thing. Somehow Jesus touched everyone in unique ways and based upon their specific journeys, yet he still offered them identical directions to be saved.

DISCOVER

Look up the following passages and take note of what's declared about salvation (and what a person does or doesn't need to do to receive it):

Matthew 7:21

Matthew 9:13

Matthew 25:31-46

Luke 7:44-48

Luke 11:37-41

John 3:3-6

John 8:31-32

John 11:25-26

Romans 1:20

Romans 10:9

Romans 10:13-15

What common threads do you see in these passages?

And what about people in the Old Testament? Before Jesus was born, people trusted in him without even knowing his name:

> Covenants established a nation. (Genesis 12:1-3)
> Laws established an awareness. (Matthew 5:17-18)
> Sacrifices established a trust. (1 Samuel 15:22)
> Prophets established a testimony. (Romans 3:21)
> God established a plan. (Revelation 13:8)

*How would you feel about having to trust in Jesus as the Jews did—
with no understanding of the Messiah's name, but by faith alone?*

Now consider the different steps we walk through in the process
of salvation.

General Awareness
God's fingerprints are unconsciously evident both in us and
around us, as all of creation points the way to God before we
even realize it. This underscores how God has taken the first step
in our direction so we can take the first step in his. (See Romans
1:20.)

Truth Awareness
As we hear the truth of God through teaching and encounter it
by reading, we begin to walk less in the darkness and find our life
becoming illuminated by the Light. (See Romans 2:14-15.)

Sin Awareness
Once people realize their sinfulness and broken identity apart
from God, they face a crisis and must decide whether or not
they'll continue on in this way. If they choose not to, then they
must repent (which means to "turn away" from sin and "return"
to God) and resolve before God not to continue in their old ways.
(See 1 John 1:8-10.)

Identity Awareness
If we confess with our mouths and lives that Jesus is Lord and
believe in our hearts that he is the risen Messiah and Savior,
God adds the final "punctuation" by making us his own. At that
time we're no longer who we were, but we are new creations,
experiencing a slice of the abundant life that Jesus described.
(See 2 Corinthians 5:16-17; John 10:10.)

Growth Awareness

The Holy Spirit takes on the role of counseling the new believer into steps of growth. In every circumstance and part of life, people must choose to either surrender to God or continue trying to control things in their own power. Every choice a person makes to open up to God allows the individual's love for God and others to grow. (See John 16:13; Philippians 2:12.)

Purpose Awareness

All Christians are given resources and gifts to help them reveal the kingdom of God on earth and invite people to respond to Jesus. From tithing to talents, the question we must answer is whether we're going to be spectators or players. If we decide to contribute, then others can come to faith and the cycle of salvation can begin for someone else. (See 1 Corinthians 12.)

Salvation contains three promises, which can all be found in John 16:33—"I have told you these things, so that in me you may have peace. In this world you will have trouble. But take heart! I have overcome the world." According to this verse, salvation offers—

- Everlasting life and peace
- A purpose in God's Story
- Trouble in this world

Which of these three is most appealing to you?

REFLECT
• How would you describe the way you came to Jesus?

• How was your journey to salvation similar to the journeys of other people you know?

• How was your journey to salvation *different* from the journeys of other people you know?

PRAY
God, you love me. I know this from your Word, your sacrifice, and your created world. I reach out to you yet again today, thankful that I can belong to you and somehow be strong when I am weak. Thank you for the renewed identity that I've received as your child. In Jesus' name, Amen.

IMMERSE
Using symbols only, draw out a timeline of events that tells the story of how you became a Christian.

Interaction 3: What Does It Mean to Grow Spiritually?

CONSIDER

A lot of families keep track of their kids' growth by making little notches or lines on the doorframe of a room. Maybe your family has done this, too, and you've enjoyed measuring how tall you are today versus how tall you were when you were younger. It can be fun to track our growth, especially when we normally can't tell how much we've changed without referring to such marks.

However, our spiritual growth is more difficult to gauge. We're told that the true test of a person who is in Christ is that she's growing in her love for Jesus and for other people. The catch is how to measure such a thing. Perhaps this is why God offered us some insights into how spiritual growth should look in our lives. Some of the best ones come from Jesus' words about the Greatest Commandment and Paul's description of the fruit of the Spirit.

DISCOVER

The Greatest Commandment

One of the teachers of the law came and heard them debating. Noticing that Jesus had given them a good answer, he asked him, "Of all the commandments, which is the most important?"

"The most important one," answered Jesus, "is this: 'Hear, O Israel: The Lord our God, the Lord is one. Love the Lord your God with all your heart and with all your soul and with all your mind and with all your strength.' The second is this: 'Love your neighbor as yourself.' There is no commandment greater than these."

"Well said, teacher," the man replied. "You are right in saying that God is one and there is no other but him. To love him with all your heart, with all your understanding and with all your strength, and to love your neighbor as yourself is more important than all burnt offerings and sacrifices."

When Jesus saw that he had answered wisely, he said to him, "You are not far from the kingdom of God." And from then on no one dared ask him any more questions. (Mark 12:28-34)

What's your impression of the guy who asked Jesus these questions?

Why do you think Jesus specifically mentioned love in the particular ways that he did (rather than just using generalities)?

The Fruit of the Spirit

But the fruit of the Spirit is love, joy, peace, patience, kindness, goodness, faithfulness, gentleness and self-control. Against such things there is no law. Those who belong to Christ Jesus have crucified the sinful nature with its passions and desires. Since we live by the Spirit, let us keep in step with the Spirit. (Galatians 5:22-25)

Love: Am I willing and able to let all I do track back to a spirit of love? Or do people feel I'm a bit focused on myself and the things of this world?

Joy: Do people get the sense that my life is brimming with joy? Or do they sense I'm somewhat bitter toward people?

Peace: Is there a sense of contentment about me regarding my lot in life? Or is there insecurity in my spirit?

Patience: Do I take the time to enter the world of others? Or do I demand that people do things my way?

Kindness: Am I known for my kindness? Or am I known for speaking against and about other people?

Goodness: Do I practice my faith to help others see the goodness of God? Or do my actions and attitudes make people frustrated and angry?

Faithfulness: Would people say I stick with God's plan—even in areas of life that I'd prefer not to? Or am I selective about which Scriptures I follow?

Gentleness: Would people describe me as a vise holding an unbroken egg? Or would they describe me as a vise with egg smashed all over it?

Self-control: Looking back at the end of the day, would I see that my conversations and thought life have included a lot of "I don't need to do that, so I won't"? Or would "That's just the way I am, so look out!" dominate?

REFLECT

- Look through the words of Jesus and think about when you've seen someone love God with all her heart...her mind...her soul...and her strength. What did that look like being lived out in a practical way?

- Does the list of spiritual fruit in Galatians inspire you or intimidate you?

- Consider the fact that *fruit*, not *fruits*, is used—meaning, Christians don't get just a few of the fruits. They get *all* of them—it's a package deal. How might knowing this change your perspective on living this out?

PRAY

Father, I want to keep growing so I remain on the fully alive path you have for me.

Cause me to be uncomfortable with comfort.

Create in me a love for the people I say I love, but don't show love to.

Inspire me not to think, *Someone else will do it.*

Deepen my understanding of you and my obedience to you.

Help me lead a person to you every day, and then please do your thing.

Show me how to help the Christians around me become fully devoted disciples.

Protect the relationships in my household with your sticky bond of love.

And bless your church to do mighty things for you!

IMMERSE

Commit to pray for one unsaved person and one saved person every day this year. Pray that God would open up opportunities for you to be a part of their lives in inspiring ways and for the opportunity to talk about your faith.

SUMMARY NARRATIVE

Take some time now to read through the Summary Narrative of the Bible on page 14 and answer the questions that follow. Repeating this exercise will help you put what you've learned in this chapter into the greater context of the overarching storyline of the Bible.

CREATION → SEPARATION → PROMISE → GOD-WITH-US → DEATH TO LIFE → THE CHURCH → NEW CREATION

CHAPTER 7

Interaction 1: What Is the Church?

CONSIDER

Language is a compelling thing. Have you ever heard of "word association"? It's a classic exercise that can be used as a fun game to pass the time or a powerful counseling tool. Either way, it involves one person saying a word or phrase and a second person responding with whatever word or phrase comes to mind first. Some psychologists believe you can tell a lot about people based on the way they respond to different words.

Many times when we use or hear the word *church*, we picture a place we can go to—a building, campus, the youth room, or a meeting space. We may say things like, "I'm going to church." This statement implies that when we're inside a building, we're "at church," and when we leave that building, we're done with "church." Without realizing it, this language can limit how we think about God...and even how we think about ourselves.

The Bible reveals that, despite their human flaws, the original community of first-century Christ-followers was a mighty movement—a fully alive relationship of "people and God" restoring each other and the world into its original image. While gathering together as the church was a priority, so was staying connected with God and each other every day. And these raw believers were working on a task from Jesus himself—to go out and create disciples in every nation. All of this is what the "church" is supposed to be.

So basically the church is designed by God to be the ultimate "word association." Jesus is the Word (John 1:1) who associates with us, and we are Jesus' "association" that helps the world better associate with the Word. But like the classic exercise, we can see this as being either a fun game to pass the time...or a powerful counseling tool—one that restores our friends and family back to God.

DISCOVER

Take a look at what the Bible says about the two general identities of the church: Local and universal.

Local Identity

1. Gathered: How We Assemble

> Every day they continued to meet together in the temple courts. They broke bread in their homes and ate together with glad and sincere hearts, praising God and enjoying the favor of all the people. And the Lord added to their number daily those who were being saved. (Acts 2:46-47)

> What then shall we say, brothers and sisters? When you come together, each of you has a hymn, or a word of instruction, a revelation, a tongue or an interpretation. Everything must be done so that the church may be built up. (1 Corinthians 14:26)

> All the believers were one in heart and mind. No one claimed that any of their possessions was their own, but they shared everything they had. With great power the apostles continued to testify to the resurrection of the Lord Jesus. And God's grace was so powerfully at work in them all that there were no needy persons among them.

For from time to time those who owned land or houses sold them, brought the money from the sales, and put it at the apostles' feet, and it was distributed to anyone who had need. (Acts 4:32-35)

To Philemon our dear friend and fellow worker—also to Apphia our sister and Archippus our fellow soldier—and to the church that meets in your home. (Philemon 1:1-2)

In what kinds of environments do you see the early church gathering?

List the reasons why you think the church gathered together.

2. Visible: What We See Right Now on Earth

On that day a great persecution broke out against the church in Jerusalem, and all except the apostles were scattered throughout Judea and Samaria. (Acts 8:1)

Then the church throughout Judea, Galilee and Samaria enjoyed a time of peace and was strengthened. Living in the fear of the Lord and encouraged by the Holy Spirit, it increased in numbers. (Acts 9:31)

Of the words below, circle the ones that best describe how you believe the world perceives the church:

Loving	Helpful	Inspiring	Angry
Growing	Honest	Secretive	Caring
"Like Jesus"	Naive	Careless	Bold
Truthful	Ignorant	Boring	Practical
Inviting	Separated	Global	Technological
Bitter	Educated	Reckless	Relational
Equipping			

Now go back and underline the words that best describe how you feel about the church.

3. Unique: Who We Are Geographically

Then Barnabas went to Tarsus to look for Saul, and when he found him, he brought him to Antioch. So for a whole year Barnabas and Saul met with the church and taught great numbers of people. The disciples were called Christians first at Antioch.

During this time some prophets came down from Jerusalem to Antioch. One of them, named Agabus, stood up and through the Spirit predicted that a severe famine would spread over the entire Roman world. (This happened during the reign of Claudius.) The disciples, as each one was able, decided to provide help for the believers living in Judea. This they did, sending their gift to the elders by Barnabas and Saul. (Acts 11:25-30)

The churches in the province of Asia send you greetings. Aquila and Priscilla greet you warmly in the Lord, and so does the church that meets at their house. (1 Corinthians 16:19)

Give my greetings to the brothers and sisters at Laodicea, and to Nympha and the church in her house. (Colossians 4:15)

What's unique about the area where you live when compared to other close-by towns?

How could this local uniqueness impact the way your church functions?

Universal Identity

1. Scattered: How We Live

> They devoted themselves to the apostles' teaching and
> to fellowship, to the breaking of bread and to prayer.
> Everyone was filled with awe at the many wonders and
> signs performed by the apostles. All the believers were
> together and had everything in common. They sold
> property and possessions to give to anyone who had
> need. (Acts 2:42-45)

> Day after day, in the temple courts and from house to
> house, they never stopped teaching and proclaiming the
> good news that Jesus is the Messiah. (Acts 5:42)

> And whatever you do, whether in word or deed, do it
> all in the name of the Lord Jesus, giving thanks to God
> the Father through him. (Colossians 3:17)

*Write one sentence or a short paragraph that imagines how you will
"be the church" to someone tomorrow based on something you
know you're doing.*

Example: Tomorrow, I will be yours at band practice, and I will
ask others what they did this week. After I listen to their stories,
I'll share mine in an attempt to talk about my recent trip with my
youth group. I hope to use this story to connect them with God.

Your story: Tomorrow, I will be yours...

2. Invisible: What We'll See in Heaven One Day

> "Sir," the woman said, "I can see that you are a
> prophet. Our ancestors worshiped on this mountain, but

you Jews claim that the place where we must worship is in Jerusalem."

"Woman," Jesus replied, "believe me, a time is coming when you will worship the Father neither on this mountain nor in Jerusalem. You Samaritans worship what you do not know; we worship what we do know, for salvation is from the Jews. Yet a time is coming and has now come when the true worshipers will worship the Father in the Spirit and in truth, for they are the kind of worshipers the Father seeks. God is spirit, and his worshipers must worship in the Spirit and in truth." (John 4:19-24)

Then I saw "a new heaven and a new earth," for the first heaven and the first earth had passed away, and there was no longer any sea I saw the Holy City, the new Jerusalem, coming down out of heaven from God, prepared as a bride beautifully dressed for her husband. And I heard a loud voice from the throne saying, "Look! God's dwelling place is now among the people and he will dwell with them. They will be his people, and God himself will be with them and be their God. 'He will wipe every tear from their eyes. There will be no more death' or mourning or crying or pain, for the old order of things has passed away." (Revelation 21:1-4)

What do you imagine this will "feel like" to you as it's happening?

3. Mosaic: Who We Are Collectively

> After this I looked, and there before me was a great
> multitude that no one could count, from every nation,
> tribe, people and language, standing before the throne
> and in front of the Lamb. They were wearing white
> robes and were holding palm branches in their hands.
> And they cried out in a loud voice: "Salvation belongs
> to our God, who sits on the throne, and to the Lamb."
> (Revelation 7:9-10)

*Write out specific things you appreciate about spiritual leaders in
both local and global communities who minister in different ways
from your church.*

_____

_____

_____

_____

_____

REFLECT

Spend time interviewing someone, visiting a library, or using the
Internet to find out answers to these questions:

• What are three things happening in your church that directly
affect you?

• What are three things happening in your church that directly
affect others?

• What are three things happening in a different church in your
area?

• What are three things happening in a church on a different
continent?

PRAY

Think about the ways you've seen God restoring your original goodness or innocence as you grow in your faith. Write a prayer that consists only of praises to God for working in your life in these specific ways. Thank God for not only where you've been, but also the person you've become.

IMMERSE

Grab another Christian friend your age and set up appointments to visit with the spiritual leaders of your church. Ask them for three prayer requests that you can pray about, and then pray for them right there. Then ask them to suggest two other churches you could visit in the area and do the same thing for the spiritual leaders there.

Interaction 2: What Role Does the Church Play in the Life of a Christian?

CONSIDER

Every year something amazing happens as new churches form in order to reach groups of people who are far from God and help them grow in their faith. This process often starts with a blank slate, as a group of Christians sits down and prays deep prayers together about what God is doing in a particular region and what it means for them to join God in his work. As a result, everything from the style of teaching to the type of ministries developed will differ from one church to the next.

There's a problem with this approach, though…and it has to do with you and me.

Just as every church has to figure out what it means to be the people of God where they live, every Christian must also ask that same question every day. Interestingly, though, we seldom do, and we settle into something "lesser." Oftentimes we'll join a church or a youth group because we like "what they're doing." But instead of praying sweaty prayers of our own, we just figure out what it means to mimic the behavior in the room. Without realizing it, we end up coasting on the momentum of the community without ever wrestling with God ourselves.

Maybe this is why so many high school students drop out of church after they graduate. While your youth group or congregation is supposed to play a powerful role in your life, it's never meant to replace your having your own relationship with Jesus Christ. He gives each of us a blank slate first, and then a dream to impact the world forever—not only with his church, but also as a part of his church. But if your whole idea of church is limited to what happens in a particular program or environment, you'll miss out on this amazing journey.

Don't settle for a lesser dream than the one God designed for your life. When everything is stripped away—the building, events, and activities—the presence of God is still with you, and you are his church! Continue meeting with other Christians and spiritual teachers who will expose you to thrilling truths in an expectant environment about our awe-inspiring God. But don't forget to also live, love, and lead in the "Way of Jesus" every day of the week. If you do, then you will "BE the church" and change the world from the inside out.

DISCOVER

Let's take a look at the natural give and take that should be present in the growth of your spiritual life and the life of the church.

The Church Plays a Role in Growing Your Life

1. Teaching You Truth

Now in the church at Antioch there were prophets and teachers: Barnabas, Simeon called Niger, Lucius of Cyrene, Manaen (who had been brought up with Herod the tetrarch) and Saul. While they were worshiping the Lord and fasting, the Holy Spirit said, "Set apart for me Barnabas and Saul for the work to which I have called them." So after they had fasted and prayed, they placed their hands on them and sent them off. (Acts 13:1-3)

Follow my example, as I follow the example of Christ. I praise you for remembering me in everything and for holding to the traditions just as I passed them on to you. (1 Corinthians 11:1-2)

Although I hope to come to you soon, I am writing you these instructions so that, if I am delayed, you will know how people ought to conduct themselves in God's household, which is the church of the living God, the pillar and foundation of the truth. (1 Timothy 3:14-15)

Think about the people in your life who have been professionally trained to do what they do, whether it was academic or "on the job" training. Make a list of whoever comes to mind:

What good can come about through people who teach the Word of God and know what they're talking about?

2. Encouraging Your Journey

And let us consider how we may spur one another on toward love and good deeds, not giving up meeting together, as some are in the habit of doing, but encouraging one another—and all the more as you see the Day approaching. (Hebrews 10:24-25)

What do you look forward to the most when you gather with your church or youth group?

3. Aligning Your Focus

On one occasion, while he was eating with them, he gave them this command: "Do not leave Jerusalem, but wait for the gift my Father promised, which you have heard me speak about...It is not for you to know the times or dates the Father has set by his own authority. But you will receive power when the Holy Spirit comes on you; and you will be my witnesses in Jerusalem, and in all Judea and Samaria, and to the ends of the earth." (Acts 1:4, 7-8)

So Peter was kept in prison, but the church was earnestly praying to God for him. (Acts 12:5)

There are many things and people that you could be concerned about and praying for in any given situation. Think about what should be prayed for publicly, though. What makes something important enough that it should be brought up in a worship gathering for everyone to pray for and focus on?

4. Maximizing Your Contribution

In those days when the number of disciples was increasing, the Hellenistic Jews among them complained against the Hebraic Jews because their widows were being overlooked in the daily distribution of food. So the Twelve gathered all the disciples together and said, "It would not be right for us to neglect the ministry of the word of God in order to wait on tables. Brothers and sisters, choose seven men from among you who are known to be full of the Spirit and wisdom. We will turn this responsibility over to them and will give our attention to prayer and the ministry of the word." (Acts 6:1-4)

Just as a body, though one, has many parts, but all its many parts form one body, so it is with Christ... Now you are the body of Christ, and each one of you is a part of it. And God has placed in the church first of all apostles, second prophets, third teachers, then miracles, then gifts of healing, of helping, of guidance, and of different kinds of tongues. Are all apostles? Are all prophets? Are all teachers? Do all work miracles? Do all have gifts of healing? Do all speak in tongues? Do all interpret? Now eagerly desire the greater gifts. (1 Corinthians 12:12, 27-31)

Are you someone who likes to do a particular task—and do it well—on a regular basis? Or would you rather use your skills in frequently changing ways?

In what ways could your resources, skills, gifts, and experience be used to change the lives of others?

Your Life Plays a Role in Growing the Church

1. Teaching Others Truth

"Therefore let all Israel be assured of this: God has made this Jesus, whom you crucified, both Lord and Messiah."

When the people heard this, they were cut to the heart and said to Peter and the other apostles, "Brothers, what shall we do?"

Peter replied, "Repent and be baptized, every one of you, in the name of Jesus Christ for the forgiveness of your sins. And you will receive the gift of the Holy Spirit. The promise is for you and your children and for all who are far off—for all whom the Lord our God will call." (Acts 2:36-39)

Then Philip ran up to the chariot and heard the man reading Isaiah the prophet. "Do you understand what you are reading?" Philip asked.

"How can I," he said, "unless someone explains it to me?" So he invited Philip to come up and sit with him. (Acts 8:30-31)

We do, however, speak a message of wisdom among the mature, but not the wisdom of this age or of the rulers of this age, who are coming to nothing. No, we declare God's wisdom, a mystery that has been hidden and that God destined for our glory before time began. None of the rulers of this age understood it, for if they had, they would not have crucified the Lord of glory. (1 Corinthians 2:6-8)

Write out four absolutely and undoubtedly true things you've learned about God that have impacted your life.

2. Encouraging Others' Journeys

My brothers and sisters, if one of you should wander from the truth and someone should bring them back, remember this: Whoever turns a sinner from the way of error will save them from death and cover over a multitude of sins. (James 5:19-20)

Describe a time when you realized someone you knew was thinking about walking away from God. (If you can't think of such an instance, describe a time when someone who knew what was right was about to do something that was wrong or sinful.)

3. Aligning Others' Focus

When Cephas came to Antioch, I opposed him to his face, because he stood condemned. (Galatians 2:11)

But you are a chosen people, a royal priesthood, a holy nation, God's special possession, that you may declare the praises of him who called you out of darkness into his wonderful light. (1 Peter 2:9)

Write the names of your unsaved friends and family members below. Then consider your feelings of urgency (or lack of urgency) over their spiritual lives. How would you describe it using one of these two phrases—"Very urgent" or "Not urgent"? (No "in-between" circles allowed—press yourself on this.)

Name: _____ Very urgent Not urgent

Name: _____ Very urgent Not urgent

Name: _____ Very urgent Not urgent

Name: _____ Very urgent Not urgent

Name: _____ Very urgent Not urgent

Name: _____ Very urgent Not urgent

Name: _____ Very urgent Not urgent

4. Maximizing Others' Contributions

Greet Priscilla and Aquila, my co-workers in Christ Jesus. They risked their lives for me. Not only I but all the churches of the Gentiles are grateful to them. (Romans 16:3-4)

For this reason I have sent to you Timothy, my son whom I love, who is faithful in the Lord. He will remind you of my way of life in Christ Jesus, which agrees with what I teach everywhere in every church. (1 Corinthians 4:17)

If you were going to share your faith with a particular group of people—at home, school, work, or wherever—who is one person your age you'd want to partner with in order to maximize your impact for Christ together?

REFLECT

- How has the church blessed your life? How might your life have been different without it?

- What is one characteristic of the early church that you'd like to see better reflected in your church or youth group?

- Take some time to consider why you may hold back from being fully involved in the mission of the church in any areas of your life.

- Everything we've just read in Scripture was written in the first century. Think about how different our world is from then, yet how much the dream of Jesus applies to our lives today. How would you rewrite Acts 2:42-47 in today's context—if you think a rewrite is even needed at all?

PRAY

God, who are we that you'd choose to let us be your hands and feet in this broken world? At times our version of your dream church can be very imperfect, but I'm thankful that you are perfect and have placed your perfect faith in our imperfections. I don't want to be excited for you for only a few years and then drop away later on. So please help me develop the kind of relationship with you and your church that lasts for the long haul. Along the way, help me to reveal your identity to the world. In Jesus' name, Amen.

IMMERSE

Write out a one-page letter to three people who've had a profound influence on you. Consider spiritual mentors, friends who've spoken the hard truth that you needed to hear, and family members who encouraged you. Let them know specifically how you appreciate them and want to do the same for others in your life.

Interaction 3: How Do I Choose a Church?

CONSIDER

You may or may not have the freedom to choose a church at this point in your life. However, someday you'll be faced with both the opportunity and the privilege of finding a community of people with whom you can live life and travel on your journey of faith. Finding this community will be critical for your continued spiritual growth and discovery.

If that time hasn't yet come for you, then it's likely to arrive whenever you leave for college or move out to work or enlist in the military.

The Bible is pretty clear about a couple of matters related to attending church. Of course, nowhere does it say something like, "You MUST go to church!" However, the Bible is pretty clear on the importance of community, being one body, sharing, giving, growing, encouraging one another, and so on.

Some churches meet in massive brand-new buildings designed for multiple uses. Others meet in very old buildings full of art and architectural genius. And still other churches meet in people's homes. It doesn't matter where a church meets because the Bible doesn't call us to a meeting *place*—it calls us to a way of life. We don't *go* to church; we *are* the church!

DISCOVER

Below are some very important places in the Bible that encourage, inspire, and challenge us to be a part of a faith community. Read each verse and then pay careful attention to what the passage of the Bible is suggesting.

> So in Christ we, though many, form one body, and each member belongs to all the others. (Romans 12:5)

As believers in Jesus Christ, we make up one body of people, and we all belong to one another.

> Even so the body is not made up of one part but of many. Now if the foot should say, "Because I am not a hand, I do not belong to the body," it would not for that reason cease to be part of the body. And if the ear should say, "Because I am not an eye, I do not belong to the body," it would not for that reason cease to be part of the body. If the whole body were an eye, where would the sense of hearing be? If the whole body were an ear, where would the sense of smell be? But in fact God has placed the parts in the body, every one of them, just as he wanted them to be. If they were all one part, where would the body be? As it is, there are many parts, but one body.
>
> The eye cannot say to the hand, "I don't need you!" And the head cannot say to the feet, "I don't need you!" On the contrary, those parts of the body that seem to be weaker are indispensable, and the parts that we think are less honorable we treat with special honor. And the parts that are unpresentable are treated with special modesty, while our presentable parts need no special treatment. But God has put the body together, giving greater honor to the parts that lacked it, so that there should be no division in the body, but that its parts should have equal concern for each other. If one part suffers, every part suffers with it; if one part is honored, every part rejoices with it.
>
> Now you are the body of Christ, and each one of you is a part of it. And God has placed in the church first of all apostles, second prophets, third teachers, then miracles, then gifts of healing, of helping, of guidance, and of different kinds of tongues. Are all apostles? Are all prophets? Are all teachers? Do all work miracles? Do all have gifts of healing? Do all speak in tongues? Do all interpret? Now eagerly desire the greater gifts.
> (1 Corinthians 12:14-31)

We are all one, and each of us has a role to play. Without each one of us contributing to the body in our own unique way, we aren't the body of Christ at all.

> Each of you should use whatever gift you have received to serve others, as faithful stewards of God's grace in its various forms. (1 Peter 4:10)

We don't use these gifts for ourselves; we use them to represent God.

> Therefore encourage one another and build each other up, just as in fact you are doing. (1 Thessalonians 5:11)

We're to encourage one another when we're together.

REFLECT

Take a moment to reflect on the following questions. Answer them now and keep them in mind in the coming days and years when you're faced with finding a faith community. Answer these questions honestly and thoroughly, allowing them to help you to get beyond the issues of comfort with a location or a worship style and into the heart of what a community is all about.

• What's my faith heritage? Do I have a particular faith background? Am I Baptist, Methodist, Episcopalian, Presbyterian, Nazarene, Catholic?

• What are my core beliefs?

• What issues about the Christian faith are essential to me— Bible teaching, justice issues, evangelism?

• Am I a formal or an informal person—or both?

- What does a particular faith community offer that will help me grow—Sunday sermons, small groups, service opportunities?

- What do I have to offer a faith community (spiritual gifts), and where is the best place to practice using them?

PRAY

Take a moment and write a prayer of commitment to God in the space below. This prayer should be a simple statement about your desire to connect with a community of faith. As you write this prayer, be careful not to make any promises you can't or won't want to keep. Also, as you write this prayer, reflect back on the verses you read earlier, drawing upon them to make your commitment to God.

IMMERSE

Sometime today ask three of your friends the following questions.

- Do you go to church? Why or why not?
- Do you think you'll go to church when you're older?
- What will you look for in a faith community or church?
- What are your spiritual gifts and what can you contribute to your current (or future) faith community?

In addition, you can drive, walk, run, or bike around your neighborhood and try to locate as many different churches as you can. How much do you know about these churches? What makes them similar? What makes them different?

SUMMARY NARRATIVE

Take some time now to read through the Summary Narrative of the Bible on page 14 and answer the questions that follow. Repeating this exercise will help you put what you've learned in this chapter into the greater context of the overarching storyline of the Bible.

CREATION → SEPARATION → PROMISE → GOD-WITH-US → DEATH TO LIFE → THE CHURCH → NEW CREATION

CHAPTER 8

CHAPTER

CHAPTER NAME

Interaction 1: What Is Heaven Like?

CONSIDER

Every fall many people enjoy seeing the leaves change colors. Depending on where you live, you might see this natural phenomenon all throughout the harvest season, enjoying the way valleys and hillsides become a unique color palette. Maybe you take full advantage of this time of year by jumping into piles of leaves or emerging from one at just the right time to surprise your family.

What you may not know is that a leaf doesn't technically change from one color to the next. It's more accurate to say that conditions during the fall reveal the leaf's true colors. During the spring and summer months, trees produce chlorophyll, a pigment molecule that breaks down chemically during photosynthesis to give the leaves a green color. As the length of night increases in the fall and the season grows colder, the trees stop this food-making process, the chlorophyll breaks down, and the true colors of the leaves emerge.

Each of us will one day face this reality on a personal level. The Bible tells us that one day Jesus will return to remix heaven and earth together, reveal the true identity of his followers, and eliminate evil forever. During this second coming of Christ, everything will change and the true colors of all things will emerge, allowing us to realize in that moment what's been buried beneath the surface all along.

Maybe that's why so many people are anxious for Jesus to come back and set things right. It's tiring to live in a world where everything looks one way but is really another. But heaven is the realm of freedom where nothing is hidden and everything is revealed for what it really is. Jesus promised us that he'd come back again, only this time he'd take things the final distance. Think about what that powerful reality means for you before you head into the next section.

DISCOVER
Take a look at what the Bible has to say about what heaven will be like and what followers of Christ can expect to experience there.

The Bible Describes Heaven As...

1. The Kingdom of God

> "'Heaven is my throne, and the earth is my footstool. What kind of house will you build for me? says the Lord. Or where will my resting place be?'" (Acts 7:49)

> I did not see a temple in the city, because the Lord God Almighty and the Lamb are its temple. The city does not need the sun or the moon to shine on it, for the glory of God gives it light, and the Lamb is its lamp. (Revelation 21:22-23)

What images come to your mind when you think of a kingdom?

2. An Era of Consequences

When Jesus heard this, he said to him, "You still lack one thing. Sell everything you have and give to the poor, and you will have treasure in heaven. Then come, follow me." (Luke 18:22)

Do not be deceived: God cannot be mocked. People reap what they sow. Those who sow to please their sinful nature, from that nature will reap destruction; those who sow to please the Spirit, from the Spirit will reap eternal life. (Galatians 6:7-8)

He made known to us the mystery of his will according to his good pleasure, which he purposed in Christ, to be put into effect when the times reach their fulfillment—to bring unity to all things in heaven and on earth under Christ. (Ephesians 1:9-10)

Do you think it's fair for God to honor the choices people make about him? Or should he impose himself on everyone (including those who reject him)?

3. A Realm of Rejoicing

Blessed are you when people insult you, persecute you and falsely say all kinds of evil against you because of me. Rejoice and be glad, because great is your reward in heaven, for in the same way they persecuted the prophets who were before you. (Matthew 5:11-12)

I tell you that in the same way there will be more rejoicing in heaven over one sinner who repents than over ninety-nine righteous persons who do not need to repent. (Luke 15:7)

People will come from east and west and north and south, and will take their places at the feast in the kingdom of God. (Luke 13:29)

Praise be to the God and Father of our Lord Jesus Christ! In his great mercy he has given us new birth into a living hope through the resurrection of Jesus Christ from the dead, and into an inheritance that can never perish, spoil or fade. This inheritance is kept in heaven for you. (1 Peter 1:3-4)

Then I heard what sounded like a great multitude, like the roar of rushing waters and like loud peals of thunder, shouting: "Hallelujah! For our Lord God Almighty reigns. Let us rejoice and be glad and give him glory! For the wedding of the Lamb has come, and his bride has made herself ready. Fine linen, bright and clean, was given her to wear." *[Fine linen stands for the righteous acts of God's people.]*

Then the angel said to me, "Write: 'Blessed are those who are invited to the wedding supper of the Lamb!'" And he added, "These are the true words of God." (Revelation 19:6-9)

Based on these Scriptures, circle the words you'd use to describe heaven:

Joyful	Depressing	Harps	Rewarding
Status Quo	Interactive	Boring	Overwhelming
Real	Friendship	Sorrow	Music
Displeasing	Lonely	Celebratory	Satisfying

4. A Merger of Worlds

For we know in part and we prophesy in part, but when completeness comes, what is in part disappears. When I was a child, I talked like a child, I thought like a child, I reasoned like a child. When I became a man, I put the ways of childhood behind me. For now we see only a reflection as in a mirror; then we shall see face to face. Now I know in part; then I shall know fully, even as I am fully known. (1 Corinthians 13:9-12)

The seventh angel sounded his trumpet, and there were loud voices in heaven, which said: "The kingdom of the world has become the kingdom of our Lord and of his Messiah, and he will reign for ever and ever." (Revelation 11:15)

Then I saw "a new heaven and a new earth," for the first heaven and the first earth had passed away, and there was no longer any sea. I saw the Holy City, the new Jerusalem, coming down out of heaven from God, prepared as a bride beautifully dressed for her husband. And I heard a loud voice from the throne saying, "Look! God's dwelling place is now among the people, and he will dwell with them. They will be his people, and God himself will be with them and be their God. 'He will wipe every tear from their eyes. There will be no more death' or mourning or crying or pain, for the old order of things has passed away." (Revelation 21:1-4)

When heaven and earth collide, what kind of "whiplash" might that cause you? Meaning, where in your life have you settled for a lesser version of Christianity that will get shocked when Christ returns?

- *Consider the grudges you hold that need to be released...*

- *Consider the "little" sins that are actually a big deal...*

• *Consider your perceptions of others that are unhealthy...*

Those in Heaven Will Experience...

1. A New Body That Will Never Die

When the perishable has been clothed with the imperishable, and the mortal with immortality, then the saying that is written will come true: "Death has been swallowed up in victory."

"Where, O death, is your victory? Where, O death, is your sting?" (1 Corinthians 15:54-55)

[The Lord] will transform our lowly bodies so that they will be like his glorious body. (Philippians 3:21b)

How do you imagine your new body will be different from your current one?

2. A Freedom from Sin and Its Destructiveness

No one who lives in him keeps on sinning. No one who continues to sin has either seen him or known him. (1 John 3:6)

No longer will there be any curse. The throne of God and of the Lamb will be in the city, and his servants will serve him. (Revelation 22:3)

Right now we have the freedom to say no to sin, yet we often choose to sin anyway. What kind of difference will heaven offer us?

3. A Face-to-Face Relationship with God

They will see his face, and his name will be on their foreheads. (Revelation 22:4)

When you think about looking into the face of God for the first time, what feeling comes over you?

How is this feeling healthy or unhealthy?

REFLECT

- What are some of the images people tend to associate with heaven?

- How do these contrast with what the Bible reveals heaven to be like?

- Why do you think people are so afraid that heaven might be boring?

- Think about the best sensation of love you've ever experienced. If heaven is a realm of God's righteousness and love in all its purity, then what might it be like to experience such a sensation forever and ever?

PRAY

When Jesus spoke about the kingdom of heaven, he didn't speak about what it "would be like" but what it "is like." This difference reveals that we can be a part of revealing the kingdom of heaven on earth even now, giving glimpses of how things are by the way we live our lives. Spend some time asking God to help your life become an arrow that points the way to heaven.

IMMERSE

We have no idea how amazing heaven will be, but we can stretch into glimpses of it if we take the time to fathom how different it might be from our life on earth. Take five minutes and wonder about it, letting your imagination run wild as you try to comprehend everything heaven involves. If it's the ultimate reality, what does that mean to everything from colors we haven't yet seen to an awareness of God like we've never known?

Interaction 2: How Can I Make Sense Out of Jesus' Second Coming?

CONSIDER

I want to tell you something that I hope you'll remember throughout the rest of your life. You occasionally may have to remind yourself about it because other Christians might try to tell you otherwise. Nevertheless, stay strong.

Are you ready?

Here it is: No one knows when Jesus will return.

While there are many views on how this will all happen, the Bible reveals that not even Jesus himself—during his years on earth—chose to know the specific details of when it would occur. All throughout the first century, his followers were waiting for the second coming and believed it would happen during their lifetime. Even people living in our own century have predicted year after year that it would happen, and they've been wrong every time.

Rest assured, there will come a moment when Jesus will come back and the broken reality we live in will collide with the ultimate reality of heaven. In that instance God will redeem and restore all things back to the way they're supposed to be, from what we experience to how we experience it. Evil will be judged, godliness will be rewarded, and the final battle between good and evil will reveal God as the victor.

It's just that no one knows when it's going to happen.

How does that make you feel? We're going to dig into this a bit more, but before we do, think about how it plays into any other ways you might be waiting on God for something right now. There are times in our lives when it seems like God should get a better wristwatch (at least according to our timetable). Maybe we're tempted in such moments to interpret God's inactivity as his unconcern.

As we're about to discover, God is never inactive. God is working off a plan that involves everyone, including you. While we want him to address our tribulation, God is more focused on our transformation. As someone once said, "If I had the power of God for 24 hours, I would change everything. But if I had the wisdom of God for 24 hours, I wouldn't change a thing."

DISCOVER

What the Bible says about the second coming and what people say aren't always the same. It can get confusing. But there are common threads throughout Scripture that can help our understanding.

The Bible Speaks of the Second Coming...

1. As an Unbiased Timeline

> But do not forget this one thing, dear friends: With the
> Lord a day is like a thousand years, and a thousand
> years are like a day. The Lord is not slow in keeping
> his promise, as some understand slowness. Instead he
> is patient with you, not wanting anyone to perish, but
> everyone to come to repentance. (2 Peter 3:8-9)

How do you feel about God when you consider that what's happening in your life fits within a bigger picture that involves everyone else in the world?

- *Consider your unanswered prayers.*
- *Consider your undeserved blessings.*

2. As an Unexpected Moment

But the day of the Lord will come like a thief. The heavens will disappear with a roar; the elements will be destroyed by fire, and the earth and everything done in it will be laid bare. (2 Peter 3:10)

How differently do you think people would act if they knew exactly when Jesus was returning?

3. As an Unavoidable Harvest

For the Lord himself will come down from heaven, with a loud command, with the voice of the archangel and with the trumpet call of God, and the dead in Christ will rise first. (1 Thessalonians 4 16)

Since everything will be destroyed in this way, what kind of people ought you to be? You ought to live holy and godly lives as you look forward to the day of God and speed its coming. That day will bring about the destruction of the heavens by fire, and the elements will melt in the heat. But in keeping with his promise we are looking forward to a new heaven and a new earth, where righteousness dwells. (2 Peter 3:11-13)

I looked, and there before me was a white cloud, and seated on the cloud was one like a son of man with a crown of gold on his head and a sharp sickle in his hand. Then another angel came out of the temple and called in a loud voice to him who was sitting on the cloud, "Take your sickle and reap, because the time to reap has come, for the harvest of the earth is ripe." So he who was seated on the cloud swung his sickle over the earth, and the earth was harvested. (Revelation 14:14-16)

One day we'll face the reality of all our choices. How do you feel about this?

Should this knowledge change how you live your life?

People Speak of the Second Coming...

While there are countless opinions about how the prophecies in Scripture will play out, there are three dominant views that relate to a millennium of Christ reigning on earth and a tribulation period where evil has its way and disasters abound.

Pre-millennialism: A Literal Interpretation of God at Work

• Millennium: Christ will return before a millennium of peace, during which he will rule.

• Tribulation:
> a. Pre-tribulation: Jesus can come at any time and "rapture" his people to be with him before a seven-year tribulation period begins.
> b. Mid-tribulation: Jesus will come and "rapture" his people to be with him within the middle of the seven-year tribulation period.
> c. Post-tribulation: Jesus will come after a seven-year tribulation period, and at that point he will "rapture" his people to be with him.

A-millennialism: A Symbolic Interpretation of God at Work

• Millennium: There will be no literal 1,000-year reign of Christ, but we're living in a general reign of Christ right now that is constantly being attacked by a general reign of Satan.

- Tribulation:
    a. The tribulation can be viewed as something that took place during the time when the book of Revelation was written.
    b. The tribulation can be viewed as a characteristic of life until Jesus returns.

Post-millennialism: A Broad Interpretation of God and His Church at Work

- Millennium: The millennium is represented by the time span between Christ's first coming and his second coming, which was understood at one time literally, but now more symbolically. Jesus will return after his kingdom has been fully established by his church.

- Tribulation: This will be a time of rebellion after a golden age of ministry when the church will draw all people and all nations (including ethnic Israel) to Jesus.

The Bible and People Speak of the Second Coming…

You're probably wondering how some of the brightest minds in Christianity can come to three distinct conclusions about all of this and what it means for you. Is there one view about Jesus' second coming you should believe over another? Or should you just give it your best guess and not worry about it?

Before you decide, consider these last few thoughts that all three viewpoints agree on:

1. Jesus is Lord. (John 1:1-5; Philippians 2:9-11)
2. Satan is trying to be Lord. (Matthew 4:1-11; 2 Corinthians 11:14; Revelation 20:7-10)
3. We are and we will be affected by these events. (Ephesians 6:12; 2 Timothy 3:1-5)
4. We have an opportunity and a responsibility. (Matthew 28:16-20; Acts 1:1-8)

REFLECT

We cannot know when Jesus will return, but we do know that he *will* return. And when he does, the final judgment of all mankind will take place in whatever way he sees fit. The point isn't if we're absolutely right in our interpretation of all things, but if we trust the One who is absolutely right in all things.

This doesn't mean we shouldn't wrestle with the Scriptures, though. Just be sure your study of that chapter in the Story impacts the one God longs to write into your life right now.

While there are different ways for us to interpret how things will happen in the end times, we each have a role to fulfill in the present time: To assist God in winning as many people as possible back to him.

To keep this aspect balanced in your life, mark the statements below that most accurately reflect your life right now.

I'd say I spend more time reading, thinking, and being concerned about:

Understanding the end times	OR	Understanding the present time
Going away to be with Jesus	OR	Helping others to be with Jesus
The anti-Christ	OR	The Christ
Who is right	OR	Helping others get right
Avoiding evil	OR	Pleasing God

PRAY

God, as we eagerly wait for your Son's return and the restoration of the world to its original condition and intent, may we strive to live and love like Jesus. As we work to be about your salvation on the earth may we be mindful of your grace and mercy. Guide us as we look for ways to reveal your truth to everyone we meet. I pray that I might be a living example of your attributes. May you be glorified in all I say and do as I await the final restoration of all things.

IMMERSE

Your view of the end times will be based primarily on how you view the Bible. Take your time going through these initial questions, then write out what you think it means for your view of the second coming.

• Do you view the Bible as the very words of God? _____

_____

• Do you tend to accept the words of the Bible as they are (literally) or through your interpretation (symbolically)?

_____

• Do you understand the teaching of your church on this topic?

_____

• Do you agree with the teaching of your church on this topic?

_____

• Do you know what you hope will happen in the end times?

_____

• Do you recognize how this hope affects your view of what the Bible says about the end times? _____

_____

Study these Scriptures:
- God's motives
    - Ecclesiastes 3:1
    - Jeremiah 29:11
    - 2 Peter 3:9

- Things to look out for
    - Daniel 12:4
    - Joel 3:9-10

- A time of great trial
    - Isaiah 2:19; 13:8; 24:20
    - Ezekiel 38:1–39:24
    - Daniel 9:27
    - Joel 2:31; 3:2
    - Amos 5:19; 8:11-12
    - Micah 4:1
    - Zechariah 14:12
    - Matthew 24:6-12
    - 1 Thessalonians 4:16-17
    - Revelation 6

- Something to look forward to
    - John 14:2-4
    - Romans 8:23
    - Revelation 21–22

If I were to describe my view of the end times, it would be this:

SUMMARY NARRATIVE

Take some time now to read through the Summary Narrative of the Bible on page 14 and answer the questions that follow. Repeating this exercise will help you put what you've learned in this chapter into the greater context of the overarching storyline of the Bible.

CREATION → SEPARATION → PROMISE → GOD-WITH-US → DEATH TO LIFE → THE CHURCH → NEW CREATION

Foreword by Scot McKnight
CHRIS FOLMSBEE

STORY SIGNS AND SACRED RHYTHMS

A NARRATIVE APPROACH TO YOUTH MINISTRY

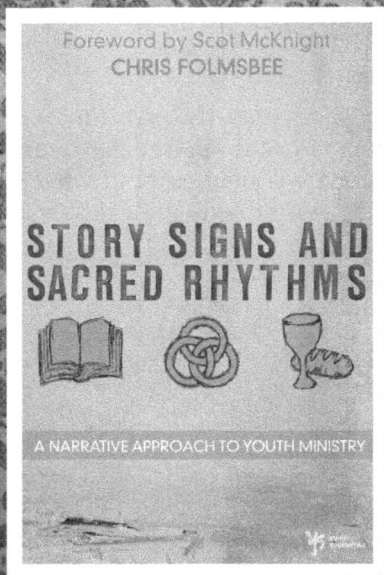

This hardcover book presents a new model for youth ministry that's relevant to the missional church and changing culture. Chris Folmsbee offers a practical approach to youth ministry that connects teens to God's mission, leading to transformed lives.

Story, Signs, and Sacred Rhythms
A Narrative Approach to Youth Ministry

Chris Folmsbee

youth
specialties

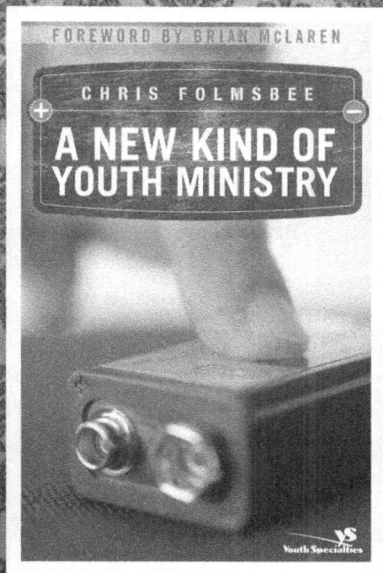

FOREWORD BY BRIAN MCLAREN

CHRIS FOLMSBEE

A NEW KIND OF YOUTH MINISTRY

Youth Specialties

A New Kind of Youth Ministry challenges you to take a fresh look at your mnistry through the concept of "reculturing"—the act of changing the way things are done or simply creating a culture of change. No fly-bynight, change-for-the-sake-of-change concept, it's about altering our paradigms for the sake of life change. You'll find that as you step back and look at your ministry through a new lens, the possibilities on the horizon are limitless.

A New Kind of Youth Ministry

Chris Folmsbee

youth
specialties

ALL ABOUT YOUTH MINISTRY

RESOURCES FOR YOUR MINISTRY, YOUR STUDENTS, AND YOUR SOUL

youth specialties

THE YOUTH MINISTRY SURVIVAL GUIDE — Kageler

HEAR AND DO — Shafer

IMAGINATIVE PRAYER FOR YOUTH MINISTRY — OESTREICHER & WARNER

BETTER SAFE THAN SUED — CRABTREE

SHAPED BY THE STORY — NOVELLI

LOSE YOUR COOL — HUNTER

MSSS :: MY FAITH — JOHNSTON & OESTREICHER

it's not easy being green — sleeth

RELATIONSHIPS UNFILTERED — ROOT

LEAVE A FOOTPRINT — BAKER

TEENAGE GIRLS — Olson — ZONDERVAN

STUDIES ON THE GO — ROMANS — polion

MIDDLE SCHOOL ministry — Oestreicher & Rubin

HOW TO Volunteer LIKE A PRO — HANCOCK

HELP! I'M A SMALL GROUP LEADER!

GOOD SEX 2.0 — HANCOCK & PO

YOUTH MINISTRY 3.0 — OESTREICHER

EVANGELISM REMIXED — RAHN & LINHART

ESSENTIAL LEADERSHIP LEADER'S GUIDE — POWELL

DOWNTIME — YACONELLI

CONNECT — MCKEE

CREATIVE BIBLE LESSONS IN ROMANS — CLARK

AWAKEN YOUR CREATIVITY — CHRISTIE

A TALE OF TWO YOUTH WORKERS — VENABLE

YOU TEACH VOL. 4 — THE SKIT GUYS

YOUTH CULTURE 101 — Mue...

THE SPACE BETWEEN — MUELLER

The complete NEW TESTAMENT resource for YOUTH WORKERS volume

UNLEASHING GOD'S WORD — Shaf...

WHAT DO I DO WHEN TEENAGERS ARE VICTIMS OF ABUSE?

WHEN CHURCH KIDS GO BAD — CHRISTIE

BOOKS FOR TEENS

MIDDLE SCHOOL RESOURCES

CURRICULUM

YOUTH WORKER DEVELOPMENT

PROGRAMMING